Christmas
with
Southern Living®
1984

Jo Voce and Shelley Stewart

Oxmoor House®

Copyright© 1984 by Oxmoor House, Inc.
Book Division of Southern Progress Corporation
P.O. Box 2463, Birmingham, Alabama 35201

Southern Living® is a federally registered trademark of Southern Living, Inc.

ISSN: 0747 7791

ISBN: 0-8487-0636-6
Manufactured in the United States of America
First Printing

Contents

Christmas Journal

Introduction

If you were to imagine a perfect holiday, you would probably imagine the people you love gathered in a festively decorated home with good food and special gifts and surprises. You would, of course, imagine Christmas.

Christmas with SOUTHERN LIVING 1984 is designed as inspiration to spur your imagination about the holiday you will plan this year and as a practical instruction book for making decorations, gifts, foods, and the other joys of Christmas. So many of the designs are easy to make; even the most impressive garland can be made quickly and easily once you know where to begin and how to proceed.

A photographic tour of "Christmas around the South" will set the mood for Christmas. In "Decorating for the Holidays," you will find specific ideas and instructions for all sorts of decorations from tree skirts to table runners and garlands to centerpieces.

"Christmas Bazaar" is filled with gift ideas and holiday projects. The recipes in "Celebrations from the Kitchen" are all tested in the SOUTHERN LIVING kitchens.

"Christmas Journal" provides space for planning. Patterns are full size and ready to use. We hope that you will enjoy the new size of the book. The larger size allows bigger type that is easier to read and larger photographs so you can see details of projects more clearly.

We are always glad to hear from our friends—our readers—about Christmas plans and projects.

Have a joyful holiday.

Merry Christmas 1984!

Christmas around the South

Often without realizing it, Southerners create a celebration of place—of the South—in their Christmas decorations. Simply by using the natural materials of an area, a homemaker will create decorations that could come *only* from her own area of the South and the country. There is a feeling of closeness to the land and an easy-going appreciation for the bounty of nature that we take for granted. Of course we use the plants, cones, and other materials from our own yards and nearby fields in

Christmas decorations, and we may find ourselves a bit surprised to learn that other people do not use the same materials.

This year, "Christmas around the South" takes an armchair tour of decorations that illustrate the use of materials that are naturally available around the South. Watch the greenery change through the chapter from yew in Natchez and broom weed in Waco, to palm fronds in the Golden Isles and magnolia leaves in Huntsville. And, since Christmas is a season in which we cherish tradition and the past, we naturally find Southern Christmas celebrations that reflect our historical background and the scenes of historic events. Houses and traditions, cherished throughout the year, are given new expression in their holiday dress of red and green and gold.

Christmas in Natchez

Think of Natchez and conjure up visions of the wide bend in the river and the high bluff above which rests the city where fortunes were made and lost and made and lost again. The antebellum South is only yesterday and you can walk through those homes built by pioneers and gentry. Time runs together, and you are only a bit surprised to find a soldier in Confederate uniform singing Civil War songs in the middle of a mauve lobby of a 1920s grand hotel; the audience, all clad in 1980s dress, sip punch and wait to begin a candlelight walking tour of the city. Three centuries meet in one place, and what remains is the magic, the determination, something of the gambler's instinct that brought people down the Trace to Natchez and kept them there. Natchez is a city of dreams translated into reality—some broken, some gloriously fulfilled—all a tribute to the spirit of the dreamers.

To enjoy Christmas decorations in Natchez, one need only take a tour of the antebellum homes that are open for the holidays. There are day tours, candlelight walking tours, and carriage tours. In 1983, no less than fourteen homes were open to the public. Some of the houses are museum houses, but many of them are homes—homes in which the owners live twentieth-century lives and preserve past and present

*Ribbon ripples gracefully over the garland above the dining room mantel of **Glenburnie**, a post-Colonial Natchez house. Wired ribbon that will hold its shape can sometimes be purchased from florists, but the owner of the home could not find wired ribbon in the color she needed. She simply taped florist's wires down the center back of regular ribbon to stiffen it. For the centerpiece, a fruit pyramid was set into the center of an epergne and surrounded by more fruit in an arrangement that follows the shape of the long table.*

When a collection is too important to be diluted by mixing in all sorts of ornaments, but you need something to fill out the tree, try this solution. The only ornaments are the angels; baby's breath and ribbon unify the tree so it does not appear "spotty" or under-dressed.

*The plan of **Glenburnie** is unusual; two rectangular rooms, one behind the other, form the center of the house and function as two parlors. The elliptical fanlight at the doorway is repeated in an arched opening between the two center rooms. Christmas decorations emphasize the repetition in the architecture by repeating candles and greenery in identical arrangements.*

together. You may even choose to stay overnight in some of the houses that are also bed-and-breakfast inns.

Only four of the houses can be shown here, leaving ten other places to visit as part of your own tour of "Christmas in Natchez." Among those ten are the house where Jefferson Davis married Varina Howell, another house so grand that the builder chartered a ship to Europe to buy furniture, a house on a hill overlooking the river and the Trace and featuring a moat to protect its back, and an octagonal house never finished because the owner's fortunes fell. Other events of "Christmas in Natchez" include a pig roast on the bluffs and an Under-the-Hill celebration with crafts, fireworks, and concerts.

*Among the Christmas programs in Natchez is a Renaissance feast. Held in the **Eola Hotel**, the feast is sponsored by the Natchez Arts Commission. The program features carols and a harpsichord, and guests enjoy a Renaissance menu prepared by the hotel chef.*

*A live oak decorated for the holidays with white lights frames **The Burn**, a three-story house built in 1832. Once used as the headquarters of Federal troops and a hospital for Union soldiers, The Burn is now a residence and inn. A hitching post (left) is decorated with a holiday cluster of pine topped with ribbon and pinecones. Window clusters of greenery are used inside and out. Indoors, arrangements with magnolia leaves that have been sprayed gold are in keeping with the formal case of the antique furnishings and frame the gardens beyond.*

Texada is a well-constructed brick building in the old Spanish section of Natchez. Built in 1792, it retains the name of an early owner, Don Manuel Texada. Now a private residence and a bed-and-breakfast inn, Texada has been a tavern, an apartment house, and the home of a Spanish governor. The present owners enhance the year-round comfort and beauty of the house with simple Christmas decorations of greenery and flowers. An arrangement of poinsettias and yew graces a chair-side table (above). Texada's kitchen decoration (opposite) joins past and present. Two platters are used on the mantel. The dish with a scene is a family heirloom. The second platter was purchased to duplicate shards of Chinese export blue and white feather-edged china that were found on the grounds when Texada was being restored. For the holidays, pittosporum and snips from a Christmas tree are combined with red bows and candles in simple arrangements to accompany the platters.

A driveway winds past trees draped in Spanish moss to the entrance of **Monmouth** (top left); though the house was named for the builder's hometown of Monmouth, New Jersey, the setting of the antebellum inn could not be more Southern. In the dining room (left), an elegant epergne is filled with cedar, pyracantha with the leaves removed, and red velvet bows with streamers (raised to the desired height with the use of picks). Mirrored in the polished wood of the Empire table and surrounded by Sevres china and Victorian silver, the simple arrangements assume the grandeur of their formal setting.

Christmas on the Brazos

Central Texas in the 1840s. The Chisholm Trail runs through a Huaco Indian Town beside a river with a Spanish name, *El Rio de Los Brazos de Dios* ("The River of the Arms of God"). An Indian trading post grows into a center for a booming cattle industry. In 1870, a suspension bridge is completed to cross the Brazos River; the first rail line also enters the city in 1870. The people who build the town are a motley crew: a Jamaican is the land developer, an Indian fighter from Vienna is the first city planner, a Scotsman gives his name to the county, and a Kentuckian operates a hotel and ferry.

Today, Waco, Texas, has a bustling population of 102,400 but the early days of the city are not forgotten. The Historic Waco Foundation, a volunteer foundation, maintains four historic houses as museum houses; a fifth is maintained by the Nell Pape Foundation. The five houses are open for tours as part of a weekend festival entitled "Christmas on the Brazos." A theme for decorating is chosen by the committees for each of the houses; the themes change each year so the decorations are new and different for each Christmas tour. The decorations shown here were photographed in December of 1983.

Fort House (a Greek Revival house built in 1868 of pink brick), followed a theme of "Merrie Olde English Christmas" in 1983. Dining room decorations (opposite) were an English Plum Pudding set in the center of a round table ringed with fruit and a mantel decorated with Toby mugs and English crackers. Stockings (top right) were hung in the English style—suspended with ribbons over the end of the Empire sleigh bed. A wreath of roses and lace accented the window in the bedroom. The lace at the outer edge was stiffened and sprayed a light mossy green; dried rosebuds filled the inner area.

The entrance to Earle-Harrison House (left) was emphasized with garlands of greenery and, on each side of the door, a pyramid of apples and magnolia leaves that stood a full yard tall.

11

East Terrace was built on a sand and clay terrace on the east side of the Brazos River by John Wesley Mann, a Texas entrepreneur who had interests in a bank, a railroad company, a water company, a lumber company, a fire company—and a brick-making company, where he instructed his employees to save the very best bricks. The pink brick of East Terrace (right top) represents the best of his brick making. Note, however, how often the words "pink brick" occur in describing other houses of early Waco. Garlands that drape Mr. Mann's portrait (above) are in keeping with the style of the grand ballroom, the last of the additions made as his affluence increased.

The *McCulloch House*, an 1872 Greek Revival structure of pink brick, was built by a merchant who married a music teacher and fathered thirteen children. It was claimed that the patina of the floors resulted from the polish of dancing feet. Note pots of poinsettias at the doorway (right). Wide ribbon runs in rows around the pots, the top tight against the pot and the bottom standing away from it.

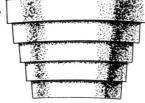

The *Earle-Napier-Kinnard House* was started by John Earle in 1858 and developed by the Napier and Kinnard families. It is built of pale pink hand-made brick. Following a theme of "Homespun Christmas," decorations involving broom weed were developed. Broom weed has been described as the scourge of Texas farmers, and there are stories of frustrated farmers even taking a blowtorch to the roots of the stubborn plant. Whatever its nuisance value, it makes an attractive material for Christmas decorations. A basket filled with broom weed joins Hessian soldier andirons at the kitchen fireplace (above). Hessians, mercenaries for the British during the Revolutionary War, were relegated to the lowest place in colonial homes; colonists delighted in scraping their muddy boots on the uniforms of the Hessians. In another arrangement, dried broom weed and china-berries circle a hurricane shade around a candle (left). The lowly broom weed has moved to the North Parlor where it rests in front of a window curtained in pure red silk and lace.

13

Holiday Customs from Nashville

Bell Buckle, Tennessee

Begin with a group of girls, all good friends who go to the same nursery school. Add their best Christmas party dresses, the promise of a real grown-up tea party, and their mothers and grandmothers to help them celebrate. One family in Nashville has the tradition of hosting an annual tea party that began as simply as this. The little girls have grown taller, as the photographs taken each year will attest, but the friendships remain unchanged. Four generations pose for a photographic record (above) of their being together for the tea party. The table (opposite) is set with party treats and a holiday arrangement. Unbreakable glasses (this is a party for children to enjoy) are combined with the graciousness of traditional pewter serving pieces, including a muffineer the girls use to sprinkle nutmeg on eggnog.

Bell Buckle is eight miles—and a whole world—away from Interstate 24. There are maple trees, Victorian houses with gingerbread trim, front porches with rockers, a main street that has changed little since the late 1800s, and a population of 493. This turn-of-the-century rail center has now become a center for arts and crafts. The quilt painted on the street is the "red carpet" rolled out for the 1983 National Quilt Convention in Bell Buckle. (The Ohio Star pattern is 30' by 50' and took seven people nineteen hours to paint.)

Bell Buckle's Christmas decorations step back to 1890 with handmade decorations, shopkeepers dressed in costumes, and costumed carolers. Santa arrives in a buggy and joins the children for a party. Decorations of pine boughs are community efforts of the townspeople, and soup and pies are served from the iron stove in the Apple Pie Diner.

Another Nashville tradition (left) also began simply. So many friends and neighbors approved of the lights strung through ivy that the homeowner has used the decoration for several years.

15

Constitution Hall Park

In Huntsville, Alabama, this reconstruction of the site of the 1819 Constitutional Convention re-creates life in 1805-1819 through sixteen buildings and their stories. The photo at right is made in the Stephen Neal residence, home of the first sheriff of Madison County. This room was both parlor and office. Mrs. Neal may have sat by the fire with her needlework and the children playing nearby as the sheriff conducted business. Notice that the mantel is black. A number of local mantels from the Federal period have been examined, and almost all of them were black—a deep, glossy black made by coating paint with varnish or by mixing varnish into paint.

For the apple string, a pick is tied to each end of a length of fishing line. One pick is pushed through the apples; the remaining pick is turned at right angles to the line to hold the first-strung apple in place. (Florist's picks sometimes contain dyes that are poisonous; do not eat fruit that has been punctured by picks.) "Tassels" of pine boughs are pushed into the apples at each end.

A wreath of greenery (left) is accented with berries, seedpods, and strips of cornhusks (wired to picks pushed into wreath). Another wreath (below) with apples, cotton bolls, and magnolia leaves hangs above toys from a shop that features Alabama crafts.

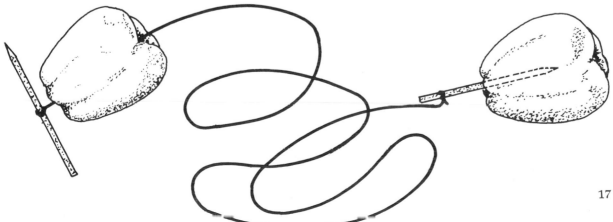

Holiday on the Golden Isles

St. Simon's Island off the coast of Georgia celebrates a Low Country, Golden Isles holiday. The lighthouse (104 feet tall) that serves as beacon and landmark for the island boasts a wreath that hangs beneath a window. Now operated by the Coast Guard, the lighthouse was built in 1872 to replace an earlier structure destroyed in the Civil War (by Confederates to keep Union soldiers from using the light to locate and invade the island). The earlier lighthouse had been built in 1810. The **Lighthouse Keeper's Cottage** has been restored and is now the Museum of Coastal History; there is no true flesh-and-blood occupant of the building, but the ghost of an earlier keeper can be heard running up and down the steps as he checks the light on stormy nights.

St. Simon's is an island of contrasts. The sea is always a presence, a background for life on the island, but the land itself is protective, sheltering its inhabitants beneath massive live oaks—oaks so strong that they were chosen for the beams of the U.S. Frigate *Constitution*. The island was once a hideout for Edward Teach (better known as Blackbeard the Pirate). The first Episcopal Church services on the island were conducted by John and Charles Wesley (before John began the movement that became the Methodist Church).

*A wreath of native marsh lavender entwined in a delicate ring of wild grapevine and finished with a bow of rose grosgrain ribbon hangs in a window of the parlor of the **Lighthouse Keeper's Cottage** (opposite).*

*A holiday wreath is suspended from the high lone window of the **Lighthouse** on St. Simon's Island (right).*

Christmas decorations in a private home on St. Simon's reflect the use of local natural materials. The contemporary house (top left) is like the island. It seems expansive with a big front porch, a gracious entrance, and a view of the oaks beyond. The house is, however, also intimate and protective with rag rugs, natural fibers, and native materials used in decorations and arrangements.

This Low-Country cottage illustrates a contemporary use of tabby, a construction material made of oyster shells and lime mixed with water and poured into wooden forms to make a rock-hard substance similar to concrete. Tabby was once made into complete walls; in the house shown here, tabby is used as an accent material behind the mantel and, edged by tile, as a floor.

The mantel arrangement (bottom left) makes use of fronds of the cabbage palm (truly a coastal plant that cannot usually be found in a florist's shop). The fronds shown here are quite fresh, but they can also be picked and trimmed while green and allowed to dry to a marvelously soft shade of gray-green. The mantel arrangement, diagrammed here, uses several pots of poinsettias with two pots standing on the mantel, two raised 3", and a center pot raised 6"; two pots are turned on their sides so that the poinsettias face the viewer.

The tree (opposite) is decorated with dried flowers and plant material: palmetto fans, statice, pepper berries, popcorn plant, caspia, and—for shine—regular tinsel. Behind the tree, a garland of greenery drapes gracefully along a railing; accenting the garland are palmetto fans with pepper berries and rosy ribbon.

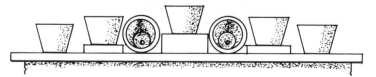

Poinsettias, cedar, and cabbage palm are arranged against a backdrop of tabby, and fans of palmetto are finished with rosy pepper berries and rose grosgrain ribbon.

*Bicycle paths traverse **St. Simon's Island,** running beside roads lined with live oaks and out to the edge of the sea.*

Decorating for the Holidays

Cast a holiday glow on your home and watch the reflections come back to you in smiles and happy faces. Greet friends at the entry with a light-hearted, breezy banner, and add a star of pinecones to your door. There are instructions on how to keep the arrangement in place on the mailbox even when the wind blows.

In "Decorating for the Holidays," there are suggestions for garlands for the stair or entry, arrangements for the table, and ornaments for the tree. For a tree skirt, grandma's yo-yos are given a new look with satin and brocade. A runner of Seminole patchwork and a cover for a card table will help you entertain in style.

Suggestions for holiday decorations include ways of using your collections and accenting your home with garlands and other arrangements of evergreen. A Christmas floorcloth for the hearth is made with stencils, and a star is crafted of wood and pinecones.

A wreath of delicate moneyplant will look well against a wall of any color, and a wreath of Fall leaves will keep its color all season.

Choose a centerpiece with golden-brown magnolia blossoms, a "pineapple" of yucca, or horses prancing around a carousel. Evergreens and berries, golden bows on a tree, and ornaments galore will all help to brighten your home and to brighten the faces of the people in your home.

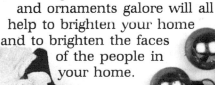

Very Personal Decorations

Collections can become Christmas decorations—even if they are not "Christmas" collections. Decorations based on collections are as personal as the collections are; only their owners could have exactly those items.

A mother-and-daughter collection (right) is displayed in a bay window. The mother's collection of dolls, saved carefully from her childhood, is used on the tree. The dolls are from nursery rhymes and fairy tales, and, since so many fairy tales are set in a forest, it seems quite natural to search for the characters among the branches of the tree. The daughter's dolls and animals are "collected" from her room to sit around the tree. They are a part of the decorations, but they remain easily accessible when the child needs a doll to cuddle or a bear to listen to her Christmas story.

Music and celebration are natural companions, and the owners of the collection of instruments have made them into holiday decorations just by arranging them on a mantel with ivy and pyracantha, persimmons and pinecones (pages 26-27).

Plaid bows are all that are necessary to dress a kitchen (below) for the season; there are bows on the molds, on the baskets, even on the handles of pots and pans.

Herald the Season

Welcome guests with a banner beside an entry or warm a fireside with a merry greeting. Banners can be made from nylon bunting from a flag shop or sailmaker or from a durable cotton such as sailcloth or canvas. For an indoor banner, you may want to experiment with the more fragile textures of taffeta or velvet.

"NOEL" BANNER

MATERIALS:

>   patterns on pages 146-149
>   1½ yards (45"-wide) midnight blue
>   fabric
>   ½ yard white fabric
>   ¼ yard yellow fabric
>   ⅛ yard red fabric
>   ⅛ yard flesh-colored fabric
>   white, blue, and black dual-duty
>   polyester thread
>   40" (⅝"-diameter) dowel
>   40" (½"-diameter) dowel
>   2 (⅝") screw eyes
>   1¼ yards rope or heavy cord
>   red, black, bright yellow acrylic paint

Trace patterns on pages 146-149, being certain to select the "E" for this banner instead of the "E" for the "MERRY" banner.

Cut the blue fabric to 39½" × 52". Cut letters, 3 crescents, 3 collars and 3 halos from white. Cut 3 stars, 3 skirts (with feet), and 3 sets of wings from yellow. Cut 3 heads and 6 hands from flesh-colored fabric. Cut 3 bodices (including sleeves) from red.

Paint features (mouth, eyes, and hair) with acrylic paints, following pattern for guide. Chin line, eyebrows, and nose should be drawn in with black paint and a brush.

Using the photograph as a guide, place letters and angels on blue fabric. Use pins, spots of glue, or fusible bond to hold in place. Zigzag around all edges. With black thread, zigzag to make line between feet and to outline sleeves.

Finish sides by turning under ½", then ½" again, and sewing. Turn under top ½", then 2½", and stitch for casing. Turn under bottom ½", then 1½", and stitch for casing.

Place screw eyes in ends of ⅝" dowel. Place ½" dowel in bottom casing and ⅝" dowel in top casing. Make a hanger from rope or cord.

"MERRY" BANNER

MATERIALS:

>   patterns on pages 148-151
>   1 yard (60"-wide) or 1⅝ yard
>   (45"-wide) white fabric
>   ¾ yard green fabric
>   ¼ yard red fabric
>   ¼ yard gold fabric
>   white and green dual-duty polyester
>   thread
>   1 yard (1"-diameter) wooden dowel
>   1 yard (½"-diameter) wooden dowel
>   5" (¼"-diameter) wooden dowel
>   2 large wooden drawer knobs
>   gold spray paint
>   rope or heavy cord for hanging

Trace patterns from pages 148-151. Notice that the "R"s are different sizes; the larger one is to be used on the bottom. The "E" is not the same as the one to be used for the angel banner. Cut letters and trunk from green. Cut 10 (16½" × 4") green bands for hanging over the dowel. Cut 2 (33" × 4¼") strips of red. Cut star from gold. Cut white fabric to 33" × 53".

Place gold star in center and 5" from top of white fabric. Place letters on white fabric, with 1½" between rows of letters and with "R" and "Y" 4" inside edges of fabric. Place tree trunk 3" beneath letters. Pin, or use fusible bond to hold in place. Stitch, using a zigzag stitch and white thread.

Turn under sides ½", then ½" again, and hem. Hem ends of one red strip, and sew (right sides together) to bottom of white fabric. Fold to make casing, turning under raw edge, and stitch. Sew red band to top in same manner.

Make green hanging strips by placing 2 pieces, with right sides together, and sewing around both long sides and one end with green thread. Turn, fold raw edges to inside ¼", and press.

Space green strips evenly across top of banner, with open end at back and folded down to make loop. Stitch along lower edge, using green thread. Make a second row of stitches ½" above first row of stitching.

The wooden hanger is made by attaching drawer knobs to 1"-diameter dowel. To do this, drill ¼" holes in ends of dowel and center of knobs; cut ¼" dowel to 2½" lengths and glue, as pegs, into holes in dowel and drawer knobs. Spray paint gold; allow to dry.

Slip the ½" dowel into bottom casing, and tack ends to hold in place. Insert gold top bar through bands and add a rope hanger.

Sit by the Fire

A warm and inviting hearth reminds us that Christmas can be enjoyed in quiet moments with a cup of hot chocolate before a crackling fire. A 2' × 3' floorcloth with a tree design can be used for the Christmas season and through the winter. Rows of trees are stenciled onto artist's canvas and sealed with an acrylic spray to make the floorcloth easy to clean. The paint, markers, and acrylic spray must be compatible. Test all of your materials by painting and marking on scrap canvas and spraying with your finishing material to be sure the finish does not dissolve the paint or marker. If the canvas is stabilized by mounting on plywood, it will be easier to paint.

MATERIALS:
    pattern on next page
    medium-weight canvas (2' 2" × 3' 2"),
      primed or unprimed
    gesso (if using unprimed canvas)
    liquid latex or flexible glue
    white semi-gloss latex paint
      (background)
    36" × 3" acetate or stencil paper
    craft knife
    masking tape
    stencil brush
    green acrylic paint
    red permanent marker (Carter's
      Marks-A-Lot® or El Marko® by Flair)
    acrylic spray (Spray-a-Rama®)

Purchase either unprimed canvas at a shop for awnings or primed canvas at an art supply store. Cut canvas, and prime it, if necessary, with one coat of gesso. Allow to dry. Fold under 1" all around for hem, mitering corners. Press with an iron to make sharp creases at edges; glue in place with liquid latex or other flexible glue. Allow to dry.

Make a stencil by tracing the pattern onto stencil paper; make stencil 1 yard long by repeating pattern. Use the broken line along center of trees to help keep line of trees straight. Cut stencil with a craft knife. Using masking tape to define outside and inside edges, mark off 1"-wide green inside border; the outside of green band should measure 31½" × 20". Also with masking tape, mark inside and outside edges of narrow green border; there should be 2¼" between outside of wide green border and inside of narrow green border, and border should be ¼" wide. Paint borders with green latex paint and stencil brush; allow to dry completely, and remove masking tape.

Along long side of floorcloth, mark a point that is 7½" inside the green border at end; mark a point 7½" from opposite green border on other side of floorcloth. Place stencil with center of trees along this line. (See diagram at right.) Paint trees with green latex paint and tree trunks with red permanent marker.

Space other diagonal lines of trees 5½" apart, aligning from center line of pattern of one row to center line of pattern on next row; turn trees in opposite directions in alternate rows, and align base of tree in one row mid-tree in next row.

Paint trees and ink trunks in border, spacing corners as indicated by pattern and setting center line 1" from wide green border. Notice that trees in the border turn in same direction all around floorcloth. Allow the paint to dry completely.

Using a yardstick and red permanent marker, draw a red line ¼" inside the narrow green border. Draw red lines on either side of diagonal rows of trees, 2" apart and using center line of trees as a guide so lines are 1" from center line on either side. Allow marker lines to dry thoroughly, and finish the entire floorcloth with at least two coats of acrylic spray.

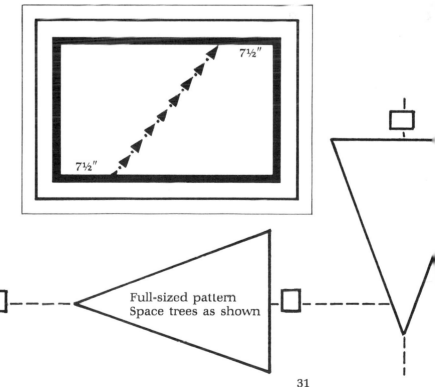

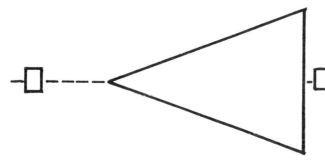

Full-sized pattern
Space trees as shown

Evergreen Plus

Christmas without evergreens would be like Santa without reindeer, bells without jingles, or turkey without dressing. With evergreens we deck the halls—and doorways, mantels, tables, and even mailboxes. Still, when the house is filled with greenery, it seems to need one more thing—a touch of color or a contrasting texture. Colorful ribbons, bright berries, shiny fruit, delicate flowers, and other accents are blended with evergreen in all sorts of decorations.

THE CHRISTMAS TREE

The evergreen most often used in holiday decoration is the Christmas tree. To the tree can be added all sorts of decorations, some of them so striking, so numerous, or so complex that the tree becomes only a background for its ornaments. Some trees, however, seem to retain more of their own character. That is the case with the tree shown here. White poinsettias set into florist's vials seem to blossom from the tree itself. The poinsettias must be sealed by burning across the ends so plant juices will not be lost; to do this, cut cleanly across stem, and hold stem over a burning candle until stem sizzles. Do not remove leaves between sealed end and flower, or the liquid will leak from the flower and it will wilt. (The poinsettias will stay fresh through a party or a weekend but not much longer.) Other ornaments are understated so they do not compete with the tree and flowers.

GARLANDS FOR THE STAIRWAY

Magnolias and pine, those evergreen staples of holiday decorating, can be made into garlands to enhance a stairway. The greenery will last longer if it is given an "in-between" period instead of being taken directly from outdoor to indoor temperatures. Condition greenery by placing it in a bucket of water and leaving it overnight in a

A garland of pine is wrapped with green satin ribbon; pinecones and clusters of nandina berries are added.

Magnolias are excellent indoor decorations because they do not shed needles or leaves as many evergreens do.

garage or cool basement; do not allow water to freeze. The magnolias are tied directly to the railing, which is simpler than tying them together and then tying them to the railing. To protect the wood of the railing, wrap it first in inexpensive satin ribbon. Then, using more ribbon, simply tie branches of magnolia to the rail. Add bows for accents.

Dip stem ends of pine in candle wax to seal the resin. Even with this precaution, do not allow stem ends to rest against a wall where resins may soil the surface; turn stem ends into the garland or place a buffer of strips of green plastic (cut from trash bags) between the center of garland (where stem ends are wired) and the wall. For strength and ease of handling, use a lightweight rope, such as clothesline, for a garland base. Wire short branches of pine (or other greenery) to rope. Turn all branches in the same direction, covering each stem end with the next piece of greenery.

The garland that follows the base of a stairway will require screw hooks at intervals along the garland; run short lengths of wire through screw hooks and wrap around rope that forms base of garland. Wire clusters of berries or cones into place after the garland has been hung. Add ribbons and bows to finish the decoration.

TABLE ARRANGEMENTS

Holiday arrangements in specially chosen containers can begin with a base of greenery. Color and texture are dramatically provided with cinnamon sticks and apples. The cinnamon sticks—tall, straight, and golden brown—dominate the arrangement in the whimsical white moose container. Shiny red apples become the "flowers" of the arrangement in the terra-cotta hen container.

ON A MAILBOX

The waxy green leaves of magnolias and holly are punctuated with red holly berries and a red bow to transform an everyday mailbox into a roadside (or city street-side) Christmas greeting. To fashion a cluster for your own mailbox, wrap two pieces of Oasis® in chicken wire and connect with a piece of wire. Wet thoroughly. Place over mailbox so wire-wrapped pieces of Oasis® hang like saddlebags on each side of mailbox and the connecting wire runs over top of mailbox, but beneath nameplate. The weight of the wet material will hold it in place. Add greenery, berries, and bows.

Cover a Card Table

When everyone comes home for Christmas, the card table is usually needed for meals and games. Cover the table with a holiday print just for Christmas or a red polka-dot that can also be used for Valentine's and even for Fourth of July reunions. The puffy stuffed bows that top the napkins can go home with friends to become pincushions.

MATERIALS:
> **3⅔ yards (45″-wide) fabric**
> **thread to match**
> **stuffing for bows**

Sizes of card tables vary; measure width of tabletop. Cut fabric to size of tabletop plus ½″ on all sides for seam allowances. Cut a strip of fabric 45″ wide and 96″ long. Fold lengthwise, and cut along fold to make 2 long pieces. Fold these two pieces in half lengthwise and cut along fold; you should now have 4 (96″-long) strips of fabric. Fold one strip lengthwise, right sides together, and mark diagonals across ends. Sew as shown (½″ seam), leaving an opening in center that corresponds to length of side of tabletop. Clip as indicated. (Figure 1.)

Clip seam

Figure 1

Turn and press, turning raw edges along center to outside. Align raw edges of strip with those of one side of tabletop (tabletop right side up). Sew, using ½″ seam. Repeat for other 3 sides of tabletop. Turn seam to inside of table cover, and sew a second seam ¼″ inside the first. Press. Place cover on table, and tie bows at corners.

To make 4 stuffed bows, cut fabric into 4 (11″ × 3½″) strips and 4 (11″ × 3″) strips. Fold the 3½″-wide strips, overlapping ends at center as shown, and sew as indicated for bow; fold the 3″-wide strips and sew as indicated for ties. (Figure 2.) Turn bows and

ties. Stuff ends of bows and ties; leave center of bow and center of tie free of stuffing. Tack bow at center back across opening. Wrap a tie around bow section, tie in a single knot, and pull into a pleasing shape.

For bow   For tie

Figure 2

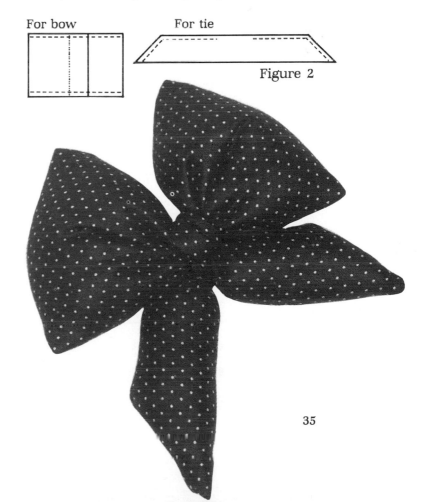

Add Shimmer to Any Room

Lucky is the person who has moneyplant growing in the yard. The delicate coloring adapts to any color scheme, and a bow of your choosing will make the wreath just right for your home. When a nearby light goes on, the luminescent wreath seems to light up as well. Moneyplant (lunaria) can also be purchased from a florist.

Separate moneyplant into long pieces. Wrap a plastic foam wreath form with wide cream-colored ribbon, overlapping to cover wreath form. Pin ribbon in place. Beginning with longest pieces, place moneyplant along outside of wreath. Push craft pins into wreath form to hold moneyplant in place. Work toward inside of wreath. Fill in with smaller pieces to make the wreath quite full. Attach a bow—plaid taffeta as shown here or another ribbon of your choice. Imagine, for example, a dark brown velvet for a library or a deep green moiré above brass and glass on a buffet.

All Season Long

For many hostesses, holiday entertaining can begin by Thanksgiving, when no one is quite ready to hang stockings or wrap presents. In many parts of the South, the weather can be quite different between the first and last weeks of December; the month may begin with Fall leaves and end with the bare trees of Winter. Take a page from the decorating book of a Victorian lady and begin the entertaining season with this wreath of Fall leaves around a mirror. The leaves have been dipped in paraffin so they will keep their color and last throughout the season. A bowl of fruit can also emphasize the harvest theme of Fall, and the flicker of candlelight will dramatize the myriad colors of the wreath.

MATERIALS:
Fall leaves and grasses
newspaper for drying leaves
paraffin
waxed paper
craft glue
strong cardboard or matboard

The Victorian leaf wreath shown in the photograph is about 16″ × 22″, but you can make yours to fit over any mirror you have—or simply to hang as a wreath without a mirror. Select a mirror or decide upon a wreath shape. Cut a mat of cardboard that is about five inches larger on all sides than the mirror. Cut out center of mat to a size that comes one inch inside all four edges of mirror. You should have a "frame" about 6″-wide. Decide upon a safe way to hang the mat over the mirror; this will vary with different mirrors, but it can usually be accomplished just by attaching a loop of cord to each side of the mat and pulling the cord to the back of the mirror where it can be taped or tied in place.

Gather Fall leaves in various colors, using whatever is available in your area. Leaves shown here include the red and yellow of maple, the brown of oak, and the green of ivy. Dusty miller leaves dry to a soft gray; a second shade of gray is to be found in the underside of the leaves. Press the leaves between layers of newspapers. Start with a ½″ cushion of paper, place the leaves on the paper in single layers and not touching each other, and cover with another ½″ stack of papers. Weight the stack and place in a warm, dry place until the leaves are dry. This should not take more than a week because Fall leaves are almost dry before they are gathered.

When the leaves are dry, dip them in paraffin that has been heated just to the melting point in the top of a double boiler (Be careful: remember that paraffin has a very low flash point and can burn easily). The paraffin will add both strength and sheen to the leaves. Place the dipped leaves on waxed paper to dry.

Glue the leaves to the cardboard base with a thick craft glue. Begin with a leaf that marks the top center and another at the bottom center. Arrange a row of leaves first along inside and outside of cardboard, allowing leaves to extend beyond the edges; cover cardboard completely.

Winter Magnolias

The materials for making these magnolias are the simplest you could imagine. When magnolias bloom in Spring, their delicate petals gradually turn to a light tan or brown, and the single petals fall to the ground. Gather the petals as they fall—before it rains on them—and re-assemble them into dried magnolia blossoms.

In the arrangement shown in the photograph at right, the flowers are displayed against a background of magnolia branches that have been sprayed with gold and copper paint. The "stems" of the magnolias can be lengthened by placing the pick beside a long limb and taping pick to limb. The containers are baskets covered with corrugated cardboard that has been spray-painted gold. Gold ribbons finish tops and bottoms of containers.

MATERIALS:
> **dried magnolia petals**
> **florist's picks**
> **brown florist's tape**
> **small pinecones (optional)**

Select one small petal and shape a center; tape to a florist's pick with brown florist's tape. Tape on additional petals, one at a time, to shape the flower. You may want to begin a center by wiring a small pinecone to the end of the pick; then tape petals around the cone. A drop of craft glue may be needed occasionally at the base of a petal to help to hold it in place. You may want to spray the finished flower with a coat of clear acrylic.

Dried magnolia petals are re-assembled into blossoms and displayed against a background of magnolia leaves in shades of gold and copper. Corrugated cardboard containers are shaped around baskets or boxes.

39

Even at night, this decoration can accent an entry; tree trimmings, pine, and magnolia are combined with red berries and a red bow.

Shrubbery trimmings from the yard and a very few lilies from the florist are combined in this delicate arrangement that tops a crystal candleholder; avoid crushing fragile flower stems against the stiff stems of shrubbery by inserting short lengths of drinking straws into the arrangement—deep enough to reach the water level—and slipping the fragile stems into the straws.

A combination of several types of greenery is topped with a bow in this greenery cluster for the front door.

Underneath It All

What does not show does matter. Beneath the pretty top of an arrangement, there must be a secure and sturdy foundation. The foundation must hold the arrangement in place, and it must be unobtrusive. The two devices shown here fill those qualifications; one can be purchased ready-to-use from a florist, and the other is quickly made.

The base for greenery (shown at left beneath a light fixture and on a doorway) requires a block of plastic foam (preferably green), a coathanger, two long chenille stems, and U-shaped pins. Bend the coathanger, pin it to the foam with U-shaped pins and secure with chenille stems. You may want to back the device with a kitchen sponge or old washcloth so stems of greenery cannot mar paint on a door.

Use the greenery base to shape clusters to hang on a door, at a window, beneath a light fixture, on a gate, or even on a hitching post or wishing well.

The cluster can be made with any evergreens you have. Use all of one kind or mix different textures. Imagine the shape and size you want the cluster to be. Place a long stem at top and bottom to mark the length; then mark side edges with shorter stems. Begin to fill in the shape, working from the outside edges of the block, and placing shorter stems on top. Add bows, pinecones, or other trims. The flowers and greenery around a candle, whether they are as delicate as those shown in the crystal candleholder or as home-for-the-holidays traditional as those in the antique spools, depend upon a simple device from a florist's shop. The device is called an O-dapter®. These are inexpensive, but florists may not always have them in stock; check with your florist early enough to allow for ordering.

Arrangements can be made in any candleholder—brass or glass, porcelain or wood, silver or pottery—that uses standard candles.

Place the O-dapter® in the candleholder. Place a circle of Oasis® (florist's base that can be used with water) in the O-dapter®. A candle punch (also from the florist) pressed into the center of the Oasis® will hold the candle upright. A candle can be used without the candle punch, but the candle may twist or become loose over a period of several days or through replacing candles.

Begin an arrangement by placing greenery around outside edges, build toward center, and add berries or flowers last; check for balance so a heavy side does not tip the candleholder.

Branches from a Christmas tree and nandina berries top antique wooden spools; remember to water the arrangement so it will last.

41

Christmas Star

Go for a walk and bring home a star—or at least the supplies that you will use to make the star. Squirrels pull away scales of pinecones, dropping scales and the stripped "squirrel cobs" to the ground. If you can find a tree where a squirrel has been feeding, you may retrieve both scales and cobs; otherwise, you may cut the scales from a cone. You will also need other pinecones,

the pattern on page 145, a 19″ × 19″ square of ½″ thick plywood, 2 short screws, about 8″ of wire, and an artichoke. Seedpods may also be used as accents if you like.

Transfer pattern to plywood and cut out star. On back of one point, make hanger by placing screws 1½″ apart and running wire between. Tighten to secure.

Beginning at the outer edge of the plywood, glue a row of pinecone scales around the star, extending the scales beyond the edge of the plywood. Make a second row inside the first, overlapping slightly. Continue filling star shape until most of the surface is covered. Using the photographs as a guide, glue 2 pinecones end-to-end along each point of star.

Glue a dried artichoke at the center of the star. (To dry an artichoke, place it in a pan in an oven that has been preheated to 300° for ten minutes or until artichoke is limp; remove artichoke, spread petals while soft, and continue to dry for about an hour in an oven with the temperature reduced to 200°.) Glue a small cone in the center of the artichoke. Glue squirrel cobs between five cobs that begin points of star. Accent with seedpods if desired.

A Bountiful Welcome

Long a symbol of hospitality, the pineapple appears as a decorating motif in everything from stencils to finials and centerpieces to gateposts. The pineapple shown here is made from leaf sheaths of the yucca plant. Spray 12″ cone of plastic foam with brown paint. Glue cone to base of wood (about 6″ tall) or a clay flower pot.

Prune yucca sheaths. Place in a pan, and dry in an oven set at 200° for four hours or until dry. Attach sheaths to florist's picks with florist's tape. Make sheath-plus-pick combinations in 10″, 12″, and 14″ lengths.

Beginning at bottom with 12″ lengths, dip the tip of each pick in glue and push picks 1″ to 2″ into the cone. Shape the pineapple as you go, adding longer lengths at center and shorter ones near top to form a fairly regular outer shape.

Trim several 10″ pieces to straight shapes, and place these at top of cone.

MATERIALS:
pattern on page 144
6¾" (¼"-diameter) dowel for
  ornaments; 12" for carousel horses
white acrylic paint
20" (⅛"-wide) red satin ribbon
tiny nail
white household glue
fabric in choice of patterns (¼ yard
  makes 4 horses)
polyester stuffing
white yarn for mane
scrap of felt for saddle
metallic trim for bridle and saddle
black embroidery floss

Paint dowel white and allow to dry. Without cutting ribbon, make 3" loop at one end of ribbon, and nail to one end of dowel for hanging loop. Spiral remaining ribbon around dowel, and glue in place.

Trace horse onto wrong side of fabric and place, right sides together, on another piece of fabric. Sew around horse on tracing line, leaving openings for dowel and stuffing as indicated on pattern. Cut out horse, leaving ¼" beyond seam; clip all curves, and turn.

Stuff firmly, beginning with head and legs and working toward center; insert the dowel

Holiday Carousel

Horses in bright Christmas-red fabrics prance merrily around a centerpiece or gallop onto the Christmas tree. The pattern is simple, and your horses can be sewn and stuffed more quickly than you would expect. Each change of fabric makes a one-of-a-kind ornament. Your scrap bag will provide an array of fabric choices.

HORSES

You may want to use these merry horses for package decorations as well as ornaments, and, for a pocket pet for a tiny tot, make a horse without dowel and nail.

as you reach center, and stuff firmly around dowel. Whipstitch stomach opening and, if necessary, around top of dowel. Draw dowel from opening slightly, place a drop of glue on dowel, and push back into place.

For mane, cut a 5½" × 1½" strip of paper, and wrap yarn across shortest side for about 2½". Stitch down center of yarn; cut yarn at edges of paper, remove paper, and attach mane to horse by hand.

For the tail, wrap a 3" piece of cardboard 7 times with yarn. Cut at one end to remove from board. Tack center of lengths to horse.

Cut saddle of felt, and glue to back; add trims if desired. With 3 strands of embroidery floss, stitch through horse's head several times to make tiny satin-stitch eyes on each side of head. Push needle through head to one side of mouth and make stitch across mouth, indenting head slightly. Glue trim around nose for bridle.

CAROUSEL

Five horses gallop through a meadow of boxwood (or cover the base with ropes of tree tinsel). Each horse in the carousel is made of a different red print fabric. The base can be used again and again. Perhaps you will choose to send the horses home with five lucky young visitors. Place the carousel on a tray or platter for easy movement and to protect the table. Streamers of curling red ribbon top the carousel and loop through the boxwood.

MATERIALS:
   12" circle (1½" thick) plastic foam (preferably green)
   14"-long section of cardboard tube
   14"-diameter macrame ring
   20" (⅜"-diameter) wooden dowel
   9" × 44" fabric for top
   2½" × 44" different fabric for trim
   6" × 4½" fabric for flag
   red curling paper ribbon
   white acrylic paint
   white household glue
   5 horses made with 12"-long dowels
   platter or tray

Paint cardboard tube white and wrap with spirals of red ribbon; glue ribbon in place. Place cardboard tube in center of plastic foam circle; twist to indent, and cut hole to size of indentation. Spread glue on bottom of tube and place in hole; allow to dry.

Cut 2 (3" × 4½") flag triangles. Sew two long sides, right sides together; turn. Turn under edges and glue at end of dowel.

Sew a casing on one long side of 9" × 44" fabric. To other side, with right sides together, sew 2½" × 44" fabric. Press seam toward narrow fabric. Turn under ½", then ½" again, of narrow fabric; press. You will have formed a binding of the narrow fabric. Place this binding over the macrame ring, and whipstitch binding to seamline, enclosing the macrame ring and forming the bottom of carousel top. Run a cord through casing, draw together, and tie. Place carousel on top of cardboard tube; insert dowel through casing at top and into tube.

Place carousel on platter. Fill base with boxwood or cover with tinsel roping. Space horses around carousel, inserting dowels into base.

Seminole Patchwork

A runner of Seminole patchwork takes advantage of color and pattern in an intricate repetition of squares of fabric. The intricate pattern, though, is simpler to achieve than it may appear. Long strips of fabric are assembled into a band. The band is then cut into vertical strips and the strips are offset by one square and sewn together. The reassembled bands are turned so squares run in diagonal rows. Careful measuring and cutting assure that squares are the same size and seams meet as they should. Cotton blend fabrics work best.

TABLE RUNNER

MATERIALS:
1 yard (45"-wide) blue fabric
¼ yard (45"-wide) black fabric
¼ yard (45"-wide) red fabric
¼ yard (45"-wide) pink fabric
¼ yard (45"-wide) green fabric
¼ yard (45"-wide) yellow fabric
45" × 15" polyester batting

Cut 2 (2" × 45") strips from yellow, green, red, pink, and black. Cut 1 (2" × 45") strip from blue.

With a ¼" seam, sew strips into a band in sequence shown. (Figure 1.) Press seams in one direction. Cut band vertically into 2" strips, measuring and marking carefully to ensure straight cuts. Offset strips by one square and sew. (Figure 2.) Continue until all strips are joined. Press seams open. To square ends of band, cut off one corner and sew to opposite end. (Figure 3.)

Cut 3 (2" × 45") border strips from blue. With right sides together, sew one strip to one short end of band. Cut off excess. Press open. Repeat for opposite end. Sew other border strips to each long edge of band. (Note placement of seam line on diagram.) Press. Cut 4 (2" × 45") border strips from red. Sew to long and short edges of band as you did the blue strips.

Cut blue lining and batting to dimensions of finished front. Pin lining to front, right sides facing. Pin batting over lining. Sew around, leaving an opening for turning. Trim corners and grade seams; turn and press. Whipstitch closed. Machine quilt down center of runner between black and pink squares and on each side of blue border strips.

MATCHING NAPKINS

Cut 12" squares from matching fabric. Turn under edges ¼", then ¼" again, and hem on machine.

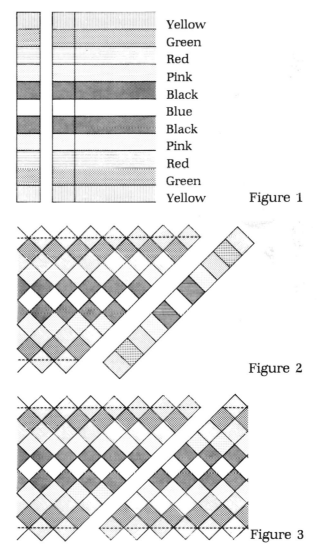

Yellow
Green
Red
Pink
Black
Blue
Black
Pink
Red
Green
Yellow   Figure 1

Figure 2

Figure 3

Fold ½" along top of pocket to outside and press. Cut patchwork band to width of pocket. Pin pressed edges together. Topstitch band to pocket along folded edges. Press under ½" around edges. Position on apron and stitch. Cut sewn band to fit bib a few inches below neck. Pin. Topstitch both long edges.

Pin apron lining over right side of apron. Sew around, leaving opening for turning. Clip curves. Turn and press. Sew opening closed. Cut 1 piece of ribbon 24" long. Sew one end to one bib corner. Adjust to fit, trimming if necessary; sew other end to opposite corner. Cut remaining ribbon in half. Sew at corners for ties.

For hot pads, place remaining patchwork bands on 8" square of fabric; topstitch. Cut 8"-square backs of fabric and 1 or 2 layers of batting. Place back, right side down, on front; add batting. Sew around edges, leaving an opening. Turn; whipstitch closed. Quilt at sides of bands.

APRON & HOT PADS

MATERIALS:
- 1 yard (45"-wide) blue fabric
- ⅛ yard (45"-wide) red fabric
- 1½" × 45" strips black, pink, green, yellow fabric
- 2 yards (1½"-wide) black grosgrain ribbon

Follow diagram on page 144 to cut an apron pattern. Cut apron and lining from blue. Cut one 9" × 11" pocket. Taking ¼" seams, sew 1½" strips in this order: black, pink, green, yellow. Cut sewn band into 1½"-wide strips and sew as for runner. Cut 2" × 45" border strip from red. Sew along one long edge of patched band. Press. Cut 1½" × 45" border strip from red and sew over opposite long edge. Press. Press under ½" along both long edges of band.

Curly-2 Wreath

If you can curl ribbon by pulling it across the blade of scissors, you can make this wreath. You will need a 12"-diameter wreath form of plastic foam, a package of straight pins, and about 350 yards (about 3 small rolls) of curling paper ribbon in the color you would like your wreath to be.

It is not necessary to cut the ribbon. Pull one length, then another, across the edge of the blade of scissors (or, if you are working with children, use a table knife). Place the curled ribbon on the front and sides of the wreath. Push straight pins through ribbon and into wreath form. When you hang the wreath, you will probably need a few more pins to capture the curls that fall. Add small clusters of red and green ribbon to accent a gold wreath.

Santa's Secrets

"Shh!" says Santa, and children know that he is making plans to delight them. Hung English-style from the footboard, the stocking is made from appliqués in bright shades of polished cotton. The colorful stocking and a wreath of stars from the same fabric can decorate a child's room for the season.

The Santa of felt that repeats the stocking motif is used as a package decoration; instructions for the felt Santa are given on page 81.

STOCKING

MATERIALS:
pattern on page 138
½ yard yellow polished cotton
½ yard red polished cotton
small amounts of polished cotton in lavender, green, blue, light pink, black, and white
sewing thread in colors to match appliqué
black, gray and blue embroidery floss

Trace the outline of the stocking, and cut stocking back of red. Trace around the outline of the stocking on yellow, but do not cut. Allowing ¼" for turning under around all pieces and following directions on pattern for color choices, cut the appliqué pieces. Embroider eyes (black satin stitch) on face, lines on chair (blue outline stitch), and bricks on fireplace (gray satin stitches). Appliqué the pieces, turning under ¼" and clipping corners as necessary, in this order: fireplace, stocking, chair, tree, ornaments, red suit, beard and hair, cuff, face, nose, mouth, hand, hat. Cut out front of stocking.

Place stocking back and front with right sides together, and sew around stocking, leaving top open. Turn and press. Turn top of stocking under ¼", then 1", and hem. Cut a bias strip (¾" × 2½") of red fabric; fold raw edges inside and sew. Attach for loop at top of stocking.

WREATH OF STARS

The simple shapes of stars and the rainbow of colors of the stocking appliqués are combined in a wreath that is pretty by daylight or candlelight and in a child's room or above the family-room fireplace.

MATERIALS:
pattern on page 142
¼ yard red polished cotton
¼ yard yellow polished cotton
¼ yard light pink polished cotton
¼ yard dark pink polished cotton
¼ yard lavender polished cotton
¼ yard bright blue polished cotton
¼ yard bright green polished cotton
¼ yard white polished cotton
sewing thread
polyester stuffing
12"-diameter wire wreath form

Plan to make a star in each of the three sizes from each color of fabric. Trace star outlines and cut a paper pattern for each size. Trace around patterns on wrong side of fabric, placing stars about ½" apart.

Place fabric with star tracings on another thickness of fabric of the same color (right sides together). Sew with a closely spaced machine stitch around the tracing line, leaving an opening for turning each star. Cut out stars, leaving a ¼" seam allowance. Clip inside corners. Turn, stuff, and whipstitch to close opening. With needle and thread, tack stars to wreath form and to each other.

Trim It with Yo-yos

Grandmother's yo-yos were usually made from calico, but these are made to reflect all the shimmer and shine of Christmas tree lights and glass ornaments. The skirt, cut from elegant lace-edged moiré, is bordered with yo-yo flowers of satin and brocade and accented with golden leaves. With the tree skirt, use nosegays of yo-yos and lace, golden bows (page 54) and tassels of tinsel icicles, and ribbon and lace ornaments (instructions on page 56).

TREE SKIRT

MATERIALS (for skirt):
pattern on page 144
1¼ yards (45"-wide) cream moiré fabric
4½ yards (2½"-wide) pregathered cream lace edging
4 yards (¼"-wide) metallic braid
¼ yard red-gold brocade
⅓ yard red satin
¼ yard gold Mylar® fabric

To make yo-yos, cut a 3½"-diameter cardboard circle for a pattern. Trace circles on fabric and cut out 23 satin yo-yos and 10 brocade yo-yos. Thread needle, and knot thread. Turn under ¼" hem and sew running stitch ⅛" from folded edge. Pull thread to gather edges as tightly as possible. Tack to secure. Flatten yo-yo.

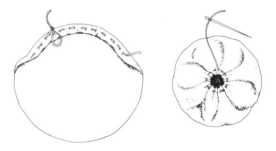

Cut a 45"-diameter circle of fabric and fold in sixths. Trace pattern, following directions to complete a full scallop, and cut out. This pattern will indicate both outside scallops and placement of braid. Use outside edge of pattern to mark and cut 6 equal scallops at outer edge of fabric. Cut a 3½" circle in center of skirt. Cut from point of one scallop in a straight line to center of skirt.

Using cream thread, zigzag around outer edge of skirt and circle. Hem edge of straight

opening. Topstitch lace to outside edge, covering zigzag stitch. Following inside curve of pattern, mark line for placement of braid on each scallop; stitch braid along line. Stitch yo-yos in place by hand, following pattern and photograph as guides for placement. Cut 63 gold leaves from Mylar® fabric, and stitch in place by machine with a line of green straight stitching down middle.

YO-YO ORNAMENT

MATERIALS (each):
   scraps of satin, brocade, and Mylar®
   **10" length (2½"-wide) pregathered
      cream lace edging**
   ½ yard (½"-wide) cream satin ribbon
   narrow ribbon or cord for hanging

Gather the 10" strip of lace edging, and draw up to form a rosette. Sew on 3 yo-yos, 3 leaves, and a bow of ribbon. Add a hanging loop of cord or narrow ribbon.

BOWS & TASSELS

MATERIALS:
   1"-wide metallic gold ribbon
   gold tree tinsel icicles
   purchased garlands (optional)

Tie bows of gold ribbon, following instructions on page 54. For tassels, cut tinsel icicles into 8" lengths and separate into groups for tassels. With cord, tie each group in center. (Figure 1.) Hang from cord, and tie around all strands about ½" below hanging cord. (Figure 2.) Hang bows and tassels on tree (with an ornament hanger), and loop purchased garlands between bows.

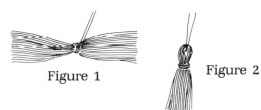

Figure 1   Figure 2

GOLDEN BOWS

For this bow, you need two people, one to extend forefingers for a bow-making frame and one to tie the bow. Children will enjoy helping; even the smallest can hold two fingers while you magically make bows around them.

Extend forefingers with distance between equal to width of bow you want to make. Bring ribbons to center beneath fingers. Cross left ribbon in front of right ribbon. (Figure 1.) Loop ribbon that is in front under other ribbon and over top of bow. (Figure 2.) Pull both ends underneath center of bow and tie in a single knot. (Figure 3.)

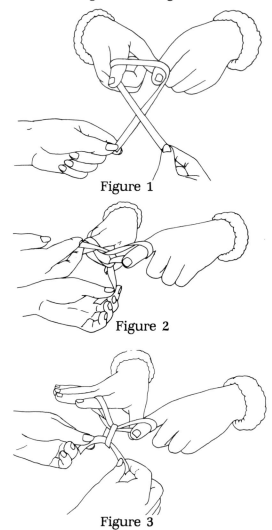

Figure 1

Figure 2

Figure 3

Top the Tree

Look up to this sweet-faced angel atop your tree. With only one pattern piece, her body is easy to stitch and stuff, and her clothes and hair are also simply made. If you like, leave off the wings and use the pattern to make a soft and lovable doll for a little girl.

MATERIALS:
    pattern on page 140
    ½ yard permanent-press muslin
    ¾ yard ecru cotton Cluny lace
    1 yard (½"-wide) lace for neckline
      and sleeves
    polyester stuffing
    batting
    ecru quilting thread
    small amounts of blue, pink, brown,
      red, and green embroidery floss
    1 yard (⅜"-wide) red ribbon
    soft knitting worsted for hair
    4" metallic trim for halo

Cut the following from muslin: 2 bodies, 2 wings (on fold), 1 bodice (on fold), 2 wreaths, and a skirt that is a 24" × 8" rectangle. Cut 1 wing (on fold) from batting.

Transfer embroidery designs to face, center of skirt, and wreath. Embroider eyes in blue (satin stitch outlined with stem stitch); eyebrows, eyelashes, and nose in brown (stem stitch); mouth in pink (outline stitch). Embroider design on skirt in green (straight stitch and lazy daisy leaves) and red (lazy daisy flowers and French knots).

Sew around body, using a short stitch and leaving open along one side. Clip curves carefully. Turn. Stuff firmly except at shoulders and top of legs. Whipstitch together at side. Push stuffing away from line marked for shoulder and top of legs; stitch on lines, and push stuffing back into place.

For hair, cut yarn into 20" long strands. Place a mark at center top of head. Draw a line from mark down front of head ½". Extend line down back of head 1". Working with three or four strands of yarn, fold strands in half and sew at back along line, with hair falling to either side. Add strands along the center line to front, tacking securely. Straighten the hair toward the sides with fingers. On one side, pull strands tightly along side of face and tack securely at point even with mouth. Repeat on other side. Separate hair on one side into 3 strands, and braid tightly. Tie off and trim ends. Coil braid at side of head, tucking in raw ends. Pin; sew securely. Repeat for other braid.

For the dress, turn sleeves under ¼" and stitch; place narrow Cluny lace beneath seam and stitch. Sew Cluny lace to neck, right sides together; turn lace up and seam down, and topstitch over seam. Fold bodice with right sides together, and stitch underarm seams. Stitch wide Cluny lace to bottom of skirt. Turn lace down and seam up. Topstitch over seam. Add a row of decorative machine stitching ½" above lace. Gather skirt and sew to bodice, right sides together. Sew back seam of skirt, right sides together, to 1" below waist. Put dress on doll and tack back of dress.

For the wings, place batting between 2 layers of fabric; stitch around edges with a closely spaced zigzag stitch. Stitch narrow lace along outside edge of wing. Quilt design by machine. (One way to mark pattern is to trace quilting pattern on tissue paper and sew through tissue and wings; tissue can be pulled away when you have finished. You may prefer to use your favorite quilting marker.)

Position the wings on back and tack in place. Add ribbon at waist and a halo of metallic trim.

For the wreath, embroider flowers in red (lazy daisy), leaves in green (lazy daisy), and berries in red (French knots). Right sides together, sew outside seam; turn and stuff. Turn under inside edges; whipstitch. Mark off wreath in 3 evenly spaced sections; wrap and shape with thread. Repeat with 3 more sections, for a total of 6. Tack bow to wreath, and tack wreath to hands.

Ribbons & Lace

Rows of twisted ribbon alternate with gathered lace in these easy ornaments that look as though they might have hung on a Victorian tree. The ornaments are made by hand and require only minimal sewing skills; if you can thread a needle and tack, you can make these.

MATERIALS:
  3″ to 4″ circle of white muslin
  2 yards (¼″-wide) satin ribbon
  1 yard pregathered lace
  wider ribbons for hangers (optional)

Cut circle of white muslin. Thread a needle with white thread; stitches will not show. Draw a circle about ½″ inside outer edge of fabric. Place end of ribbon, right side up, at right angles to circle and tack. (Figure 1.) Turn ribbon back toward line and place it parallel to other end of ribbon, with right side still up. The ribbon will make a pointed, puffy turn. Tack ribbon in place. (Figure 2.)

Turn ribbon back on itself; this time the wrong side will be up. Tack ribbon in place. (Figure 3.) Make this loop in same way as first, but wrong-side-up on both sides. (Figure 4.) Continue to make loops around circle. Draw another circle ⅜″ to ½″ inside the first, and make another row of ribbon twists. Continue to make circles of ribbon until you reach center. Tuck lace between rows of ribbon and tack.

Finish with gathered ribbon or lace in the center; add loops or strands of ribbon to vary the designs.

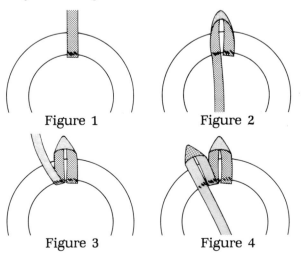

Figure 1   Figure 2

Figure 3   Figure 4

Christmas Bazaar

Here is help for Santa's helper: the practical how-tos you need to make your gifts special and personal, plus instructions for new ornaments, stockings, toys, and wraps. Choose the gifts you want to make, and get a head start on Christmas.

Cross-stitch a reindeer. Knit a gingerbread boy. Appliqué a cat on a pillow. Share a bread-dough project with a child. Build a wooden box and paint a goose on each side. Dress a Victorian doll. Sew sacks to hold special gifts. Paint a teddy bear on a lid for a cookie jar. Cut meat trays into stamps for making holiday paper. Make a quick-and-easy bird feeder. Glue rosebuds to a bell and bows to a pinecone. Fill a tea strainer with potpourri. Paint tiny angels. Stuff a boat for a little boy's tree. Make a dolly in a bed for a package tie. Make an angel small enough to fit in a walnut. Give the children some felt and glue and let them make ornaments for the tree and napkin rings for the Christmas-morning breakfast table. Give yourself the pleasure of creating something special for someone special.

In "Christmas Bazaar," instructions are given for all these projects. Patterns, if they are needed, are given in the back of the book—full size and ready to trace.

Cuddle-Up with a Pillow

Brighten your guest room for the holidays with this cheerful green-eyed cat. The two versions of the pillow shown here demonstrate how easily the pillow can be adapted to any color scheme. Choose only two colors (one for the bed and one for the ribbon), and the lounging cat will be a part of your room. Are you looking for gift ideas? Count your friends who like cats. If you have difficulty finding the polished cotton in colors you like, look in the drapery department for solid-colored chintz which is similar in appearance.

MATERIALS:
>   patterns on pages 142-145
>   1½ yards white polished cotton
>   ½ yard polished cotton for "bed"
>   (light pink or bright pink are
>   shown in photographs)
>   ¼ yard polished cotton for bow,
>   streamers and bed outline (teal
>   blue and bright green are the
>   colors shown in the photographs)
>   green, light pink, bright pink, brown,
>   gray and black embroidery floss
>   16"-square pillow form

Follow instructions given on page 142 to assemble the complete pattern, and trace individual pattern pieces. Cut 2 (17"-square) pieces of white polished cotton for front and back of pillow; follow the cutting diagram at left to conserve fabric and to assure that you can cut ruffle in only two pieces.

Cut 1 "bed" section (allowing ¼" seam) and sew in place with a running stitch (raw edges will be covered by outlines). Cut outlines for "bed" section, being careful to add seam allowances. Pin in place and appliqué, clipping curves and turning under ¼" as you sew.

Mark outlines of cat and embroidery details on white fabric. Using 2 strands of floss,

Light pink and teal blue are chosen to repeat the pastels of a pink comforter.

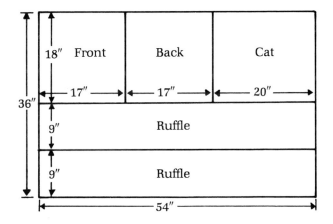

Change only two colors and match any room. Bright green in the cat's fancy bow picks up green in pillow shams and striped comforter, and deep, strong pink balances the green.

embroider eyes in black and green satin stitch with a gray outline stitch at top. Work curve of nose and whiskers with outline stitch in brown. Satin stitch a pink nose and bright pink mouth. Satin stitch paws in light pink, and make French knots (brown) along curves of body and on bow.

Allowing for ¼" seams, cut out parts of cat (head, body, and tail) and pin in place. Appliqué first the head and tail, then the body. Cut bow and streamers (to both, add ¼"

seam allowances). Add French knots and appliqué in place.

Cut two 9" × 54" ruffles from white; sew ends together. Fold lengthwise and press. Gather raw edges and pin to front of pillow, matching raw edges and turning ruffle to inside. Sew in place. Place pillow front on pillow back and sew together along previous seam, leaving an opening along one side. Turn and press. Place pillow form inside and slipstitch closed.

Potpourri & Pinecones

Sophisticated and simple—so often the two words go together. Each of these ornaments represents a sophisticated design that uses simple materials. Make one for yourself, or make enough to give as gifts to members of your club or other favorite groups of people.

Vary the designs of all three ornaments with the addition of statice, baby's breath, or bits of eucalyptus at the top. Make a series of the ornaments with white or blue ribbons instead of the red shown here.

BELL ORNAMENT

MATERIALS:
    1 (3"-diameter) gold bell
    6" gold cord
    1 yard (⅛"-wide) maroon velvet
        ribbon
    thick craft glue or hot glue gun and
        glue
    dried rosebuds (can be purchased in
        some craft stores and at potpourri
        counters of holiday bazaars)
    dried statice

Tie a loop of gold cord through hanger at top of bell and tie into a loop. Make a bow from ribbon. Glue ribbon to top of bell. Glue rosebuds and dried statice at top of bell. For variety, change ribbons and substitute other dried flowers.

PINECONE ORNAMENT

MATERIALS:
    small pinecone
    3" gold cord for hanger
    ⅔ yard (¼"-wide) gold ribbon
    bits of statice, seedpods, etc.
    thick craft glue or hot glue gun and
        glue

Shape gold cord into a loop and glue ends to top of cone. Make a bow of ribbon and glue to top of cone. Glue on assorted dried flowers and small seedpods.

BIG RED STRAWBERRY

MATERIALS:
    tea ball
    ruby-red enamel spray paint
    tiny imitation pearls
    white household glue
    1 tablespoon potpourri
    strip of gold foil paper
    gold foil stars
    18" narrow ruby-red satin ribbon
    1 yard narrow gold ribbon
    green silk leaves

Paint tea ball with enamel spray paint. Allow to dry. Glue a few seed pearls in irregularly spaced holes of the tea ball. Place potpourri in tea ball. Glue a strip of gold foil paper around edge of lid; add stars over strip. Loop narrow red ribbon through top of tea ball; tie into a loop, and add foil stars to ends of ribbon. Glue leaves to top of "strawberry," and add bow of gold ribbon.

A Simple Story

When children draw Christmas scenes, they draw Santa and trees—and the manger scene. When they are given dough to work with, they often try to shape manger scenes.

Dough is one of the most popular craft substances used for Christmas projects, and it has been used to make all sorts of small ornaments. When it is used to make figures, though, the results can be disappointing because it is so difficult to maintain shapes while the figures dry. These figures will work because they are fairly flat and thin, they are linked by slight overlapping to strengthen the parts, and they are supported by easels or baskets.

MATERIALS:
>   **4 cups plain flour**
>   **1 cup plain salt**
>   **1½ cups water (approximately)**
>   **white household glue**
>   **water color paints**
>   **clear enamel sealer**
>   **aluminum foil**
>   **flat basket or tray (for larger scene)**
>   **fabric for lining basket (for larger scene)**

Mix flour, salt, and water to a stiff consistency. Knead for ten minutes; the texture will change from grainy to smooth. (This amount of dough will make 2 to 3 nativity scenes.) Keep dough covered with plastic, and use it while it is fresh.

To shape the small scene, begin by making the base; shape a cylindrical bit of dough and press to flatten slightly. Shape other pieces to make the bases for the bodies of Mary and Joseph. Shape heads for the two. Strengthen the composition by positioning the figures so the scene is joined. Joseph's arm can run alongside Mary's cloak; garments can touch at the hem.

Add other elements to the composition: cloaks, arms, feet, hair. Shape the Babe and place in Mary's arms. Push dough through a strainer to make hair. For eyes and mouth, shape holes with a toothpick. Add tiny balls of dough for noses. Sculpt the clay figures until you are pleased with the composition. With a small brush and water, go back through the steps of the scene and moisten the parts so they will stick together. When you add small parts, touch them to a wet washcloth in a saucer to moisten them.

For the larger scene, select the basket or tray that you will use. Cut a piece of aluminum foil to fit the basket. Place the foil on a cookie sheet as a pattern for the size of the scene.

Shape the framing pieces first and arrange them on the foil: the base strip (covered with "hay" from a strainer or garlic press), the side and roof of the stable, the tree trunk and tree top. Be sure the parts touch each other.

Add the figures, building them from simple round and oval shapes as before. Arrange the figures so they touch the frame and other figures. The three angels touch each other, the roof, and the star. Note that the manger in the center touches the cloaks of Mary and Joseph. The animals are simply shaped from ovals of dough with small balls for eyes and ears.

When you are pleased with the arrangement, dampen the overlapping and touching areas of dough.

For both scenes, bake at 350° for one hour or until the thickest part is completely dry and hard.

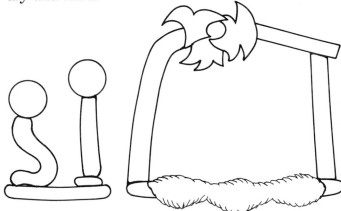

Notice that the elements of this scene are joined for strength; the basket that frames the scene also supports the back.

Paint with water color paints. (Do not use tempera; it will look just as well when you are painting, but it will become very harsh and glaring after it is sprayed with a sealer.) Allow paint to dry.

After painting, spray with clear enamel sealer. Be sure to spray from all angles at least four times so no moisture can penetrate to the dough.

Mount the small scene on an easel. For the large scene, glue fabric lining into the basket, and glue scene to fabric; dry thoroughly before hanging.

If a small scene is supported by an easel, the figures need not be thick and difficult to dry.

Displaying Small Wreaths

Small, delicate wreaths are irresistible when you are shaping your own or passing them in a booth at a crafts fair. But when you have the wreath in your room, it can seem lost. Group small wreaths, perhaps with a small flower arrangement, into a larger vignette for a dresser top or a bedside table.

The wreath on the stand is made with Spanish moss, white and pink amaranth, and strawflowers. The wreath that hangs on the wall has cudweed (rabbit tobacco) wrapped with ⅛"-wide purple ribbon. For either wreath, make a base of vines by wrapping into a wreath shape, or make a wire base by shaping 20-gauge wire into 3" and 5" circles. Place 3" circle inside other, and place masking tape over the two pieces, shaping tape to follow wire circles. Turn so sticky side of tape is up. Cover either tape or vine wreath with glue. Press base material (Spanish moss for wreath on stand or cudweed for hanging wreath) onto glue; allow the glue to dry.

Apply other flowers as desired; allow glue to dry. Spray with hair spray to preserve flowers. Add ribbons as desired.

Angels of Paper or Wood

Fill your tree with small, delicately colored angels that can be made from either paper or wood. The angel in pink in center and the angel in white at left of photograph are made of paper; the others are made of wood. As you can see, both paper and wooden angels are cut, given a coat of paint, and finished with simple details. Halos that slip onto string or ornament hangers give a three-dimensional aspect to the angels.

MATERIALS:
    pattern on page 142
    posterboard or ⅛"- to ¼"-thick wood
       (bass, buckeye, or other wood with
       low grain)
    sandpaper (for wood)
    small scissors or craft knife (for
       paper)
    acrylic paints
    thread or ornament hanger

For the paper angels, transfer pattern to posterboard, and cut out. Cut 1" circle for halo. Following the photographs, paint angels with acrylic paint, matching color of halo to color of robe; two coats of paint may be needed to cover well. (Flesh color can be mixed from white and burnt sienna; hair color, from white and burnt umber.) To paint features, dip a toothpick into burnt umber that has been thinned slightly; touch features lightly onto angel.

Thread a needle; double thread and knot. Thread through top of head and halo; knot to form hanging loop.

For the wooden angels, transfer pattern to wood. Cut with jigsaw or band saw. Sand rough edges. Paint as described for paper angels.

Fashion a loop from a paper clip and press into top of head. Attach thread or ornament hanger. Make hole in center of halo, and slip onto thread or hanger.

This is Victoria

It is easy to love Victoria's sweet face, braids with red ribbon, and fancy holiday dress. Her legs and arms bend so she can be posed. To decorate a "house" for Victoria, place her on a shelf or wrap the outside of a box with gift wrap and line the inside with wallpaper (or striped gift wrap). Instructions are given for her bed and tree. Her "trunk" is a jewelry box, and pictures cut from gift wrap are backed with construction paper.

MATERIALS:
   pattern on page 154
   ⅓ yard flesh cotton-polyester fabric
   scrap of black fabric for shoes
   pink, brown, flesh embroidery floss
   3 yards (4-ply) yellow knitting yarn
   1 yard (⅛"-wide) red satin ribbon
   ¼ yard white cotton-polyester fabric
   1¼ yards (⅜"-wide) pregathered lace
   ¼ yard plaid taffeta
   4" × 6" sheer white fabric
   ½ yard (¼"-wide) red satin ribbon
   8 inches (1"-wide) pregathered lace
   polyester stuffing

Trace patterns for body, arm, and leg (along sewing lines), and cut out paper patterns. Trace twice around arm patterns onto wrong side of flesh-colored fabric; place right sides together on another thickness of fabric, and sew around seam line with a short machine stitch. Cut out arms, leaving ¼" beyond seam and clipping at curves. Turn and stuff arms. Sew across elbows as indicated on pattern.

Trace around head-and-body pattern on wrong side of flesh-colored fabric. Place on second piece of fabric, right sides together. Pin arms, turning inward and with thumbs turned up, between body pieces at shoulders. Leaving bottom open, sew around head-and-body, catching arms in position as you sew. Cut out, leaving ¼" of fabric beyond seam. Clip curves, turn, and stuff.

For legs, cut a 2" × 8" strip of black fabric and a 6" × 8" piece of flesh-colored fabric. Place black strip, right side down, on the larger strip, placing edge of black fabric 1¾" from edge of lighter fabric. Sew ¼" from edge of black fabric. (Figure 1.) Turn down black fabric so ends of both strips are even. Fold fabric in half, right sides together, and trace patterns for legs onto fabric twice. (Figure 2.) Sew around seam lines, trim, turn, and stuff. Sew across legs at knees. Turn under bottom of body ¼". Pin tops of legs between front and back of body, and sew across bottom of body.

For the face, make French knots (brown eyes and flesh-colored nose), using 3 strands of embroidery floss. Again using 3

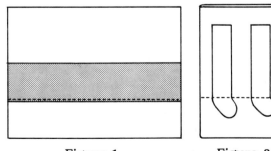

Figure 1   Figure 2

strands of floss, use an outline stitch (very short stitches) to embroider a pink mouth and flesh-colored eyebrows. Add rosy cheeks with a pink crayon.

To make the hair, thread 1½ yards (4-ply) yarn through a large darning needle and knot end of yarn. Insert needle through back of doll's head, and bring out at right side at the point marked at side of head. Satin stitch between top and bottom of back of head until back of head is covered with vertical stitches. (Figure 3.) Make satin stitches on the front of the head from the part to the sides, placing the ends of the stitches at the top and sides of the head very close to the tops of the back stitches; no fabric should show along the top of the head. (Figure 4.) Take one vertical stitch to cover the part. Push needle out through side of head.

Cut 2 (24"-long) pieces of yarn. Fold in half, then into thirds. Cut 2 (16"-long) pieces of ⅛"-wide red ribbon. Fold ribbon in half, then in half again. Join ribbon and yarn at folded ends and stitch to doll's head as shown. (Figure 5.) Repeat for other side of doll's head.

Cut ends of loops of yarn and ribbons. Separate into groups of 2 yarns and 1 ribbon (there should be one extra piece of ribbon). Braid each group of 2 yarns and 1 ribbon; turn each braid up in a loop and sew end in place. Wrap remaining ribbon around top of braids and stitches, shape ribbon into a tiny bow, and tack in place. (Figure 6.)

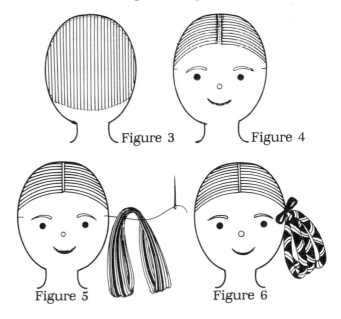

Figure 3

Figure 4

Figure 5

Figure 6

For bloomers, cut from white fabric. With right sides together, stitch side seams, ending 1″ lower on one side. Sew (⅜″-wide) lace along bottom of each leg. Stitch inside seam. Turn right side out. Hem top edge. Pull bloomers onto doll and stitch opening closed. Run a gathering stitch around each leg of bloomers. Pull thread tight and knot.

For petticoat, cut from white fabric. Sew pregathered (⅜″-wide) lace to bottom of petticoat. Turn under waistline ¼″ and hem. Fold petticoat with right sides together and stitch seam to within 1″ of top. Turn right side out and put on doll. Handstitch closed at waist.

For dress, cut a bodice using pattern. Cut a skirt that measures 8″ × 24″. Turn neck edge under and hem. Stitch lace along bottom edge of sleeve. With right sides together, stitch underarm seams in bodice. Hem one long side of skirt. Cut apron and hem two sides and bottom. Run a gathering stitch along top of apron and long unfinished edge of the skirt. Pull up gathers in apron and skirt to fit bodice. Center apron on front of bodice and pin in place, right sides together. Pin skirt to bodice, right sides together, and sew waistline seam. Sew back of skirt to within 1″ of waistline seam. Slip dress on doll and tack opening. Run gathering stitch by hand around sleeves at wrist line. Pull tight and fasten off. Find center of ¼″-wide ribbon and tack to dress at center front of waistline. Make bow at back. Gather (1″-wide) lace and tack at neck.

For the bed, select a shoe box that is a little longer than the doll. Slit the corners of the box halfway to the bottom. (Figure 7.) Cut corners from one end (for foot of bed). Using plastic foam or other packing, fill box halfway—to the line made by cuts in corners. Fold top half of box sides over packing. (Figure 8.) Remove sides from box top and cut in half across the shortest dimension. Cut corners to match foot of bed. Place one piece of the boxtop inside the end of the box and one piece outside the end. (Figure 9.) Secure in place with masking tape. Tape

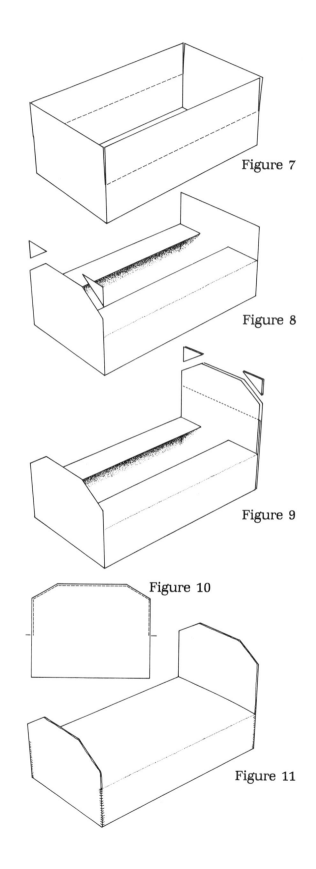

Figure 7

Figure 8

Figure 9

Figure 10

Figure 11

tightly around the box with masking tape to hold the "bed" shape.

Using the ends of the box as guides, cut two pieces of fabric ½" larger on each side than the foot and two pieces ½" larger than the head of the bed. With right sides together, sew ¼" from edges above height of bed. (Figure 10.) Turn, pull over ends of bed, tucking the inside fabric into the bed. Measure a piece of fabric that will wrap both sides of bed and top of bed plus ½" at each end and 1" on each side. Cut fabric, wrap over sides and top of bed, and tape the extra 1" on each side to bottom of bed. Turn under ½" at top and bottom of bed. Whipstitch sides to *outside* of head and foot coverings. (Figure 11.) Turn under ends of head and foot and tape in place.

For a simple mattress, cut fabric 1" longer than the bed and 2" wider. Fold in half. Sew, turn, and stuff. Make a simple bedspread (fabric the size of top of bed plus a ruffle); add a pillow and other flourishes.

For the Christmas tree, dip stem ends of plastic berries into glue and push halfway into a brush tree. Add a dot of glue to the back of gold foil stars, and place on tree. Finish with a garland of narrow ribbon.

Frame Your Favorites

Snapshots and Santashots find a spot of their own in a festive cross-stitched frame.

MATERIALS:
 chart on page 153
 mat board for front, back, and stand
 Ribband®
 red and green embroidery floss
 polyester batting
 fabric to cover frame
 white household glue
 braid or cord

Decide overall size and size of opening you will need for your frame. Cut 2 pieces Ribband® 3" longer than width of frame. Center designs on the pieces, and cross-stitch. Cut mat board with an opening for front, a solid piece for back, and a (2" × 4") piece for a stand.

Cut batting to same size as board for front; glue to mat board. Cut fabric 2" longer and wider than mat board. Wrap across front of board to back, turning 1" to back on each side; glue in place. From the back, mark the outline of opening onto fabric. Cut a slit in center of opening and trim to 1" inside board. Clip as needed for corners or curves, and pull fabric to inside back. Glue in place. Glue braid or cord around edge of opening. Cover board for back, turning edges to inside. Cover board for stand; place against back of frame, and sew in place across top of stand. Glue ribbon or cord to inside of stand and back of board to keep the stand from collapsing. Place the strips of cross-stitch above and below the opening for photograph; pull ends to back, and glue in place. Glue front to back around sides and bottom. Slip photograph into frame from top.

Your Personal Stamp

Design your own packages with easy-to-make stamps cut from plastic foam meat trays. Trace patterns (page 145) and transfer to meat tray. Using craft knife, cut out design; glue one end of spool to the back for a handle. Press stamp into paint, then onto paper. (Use acrylic paints; tempera will not adhere to foam.) Stamp paper before wrapping gift, or wrap gift first and press stamps directly on package.

Cross-Stitch on Stockings

Personalize this stocking that features cross-stitch and a cheerful patchwork of Christmas fabrics. Work the cross-stitch elements, blend a stripe and a print, and assemble this very personal gift for a friend or relative. Vary the fabrics to fill a mantel with stockings for all members of the family.

MATERIALS (for each stocking):
  patterns on pages 152-153
  charts on pages 152-153
  30″ × 7″ white #14 Aida cloth
  1 skein embroidery floss in red,
    medium green, and dark green
  ½ yard each red, white cotton twill
  ½ yard striped cotton fabric
  ⅓ yard cotton fabric in small print
  ⅝ yard (⅛″-wide) red satin ribbon
  ½ yard polyester batting

Work wreath (3 strands of floss) in center of 4″ square of Aida; mark off Aida for toe, according to pattern, and work holly design. Cut a 20″ × 5″ cuff of Aida, and work holly designs. Center name on front of cuff.

Cut 9 (4″) striped squares and 8 (4″) printed squares. Using ½″ seams, assemble fabric and Aida. (See below.) Follow pattern to mark patchwork stocking front; sew toe to patchwork. Cut front. Cut 2 white twill, 1 red twill, and 2 batting to match front.

Layer patchwork, 1 batting, and 1 white fabric. Pin. Machine quilt along seams of patchwork. For back, layer red twill, batting, and white twill. Machine quilt in squares. Place front and back with right sides together and sew around stocking, leaving top open. Zigzag to finish edges. Turn.

For cuff, cut 20″ × 5″ white twill lining. Cut strip of print or stripe (3″ × 54″) for ruffle. Fold lengthwise and press. Gather along raw edges. Place ruffle between bottom of Aida and twill. Sew (½″ seam); turn and press. Sew ribbon along edge. Fold cuff right sides together; sew side. Turn. Cut a 2″ × 20″ facing (match ruffle). Slip cuff onto stocking and pin. Using a ½″ seam, sew cuff to stocking. Place facing, right side down, along top of stocking and cuff; sew on top of other seam. Fold facing over top of cuff; turn under ½″, and whip inside stocking. Double fold 1″ × 5″ red twill and stitch for hanger. Tack inside the cuff.

Gingerbread Boy

After all the other Gingerbread Men have been eaten, this friendly fellow will still be in fine fettle. Spend a couple of evenings with knitting needles to give hours of pleasure to a child.

MATERIALS:
2-ounces 4-ply brown knitting yarn
polyester stuffing
bits of black, red, and white yarn

Terms: st (stitch); K (knit); P (purl); inc (increase); dec (decrease); stockinette (K one row, P one row).

Left foot: Cast on 6 st. Knit the first row inc in first and last st. P back. Place safety pin or marker to indicate outer foot. Repeat these 2 rows until there are 14 st on needle.

K 1 row inc on st at end (inner foot) (15 st). P row. Bind off 2 stitches at beginning of the K row. P row.

Dec 1 st at beginning of the K row. P back. Dec 1 at beginning of K row (11 st). Continue K 1 row, P 1 row until piece measures 4 inches from bottom of foot, ending with P row. Place these stitches on holder to be picked up later.

Right foot: Cast on 6 st. P first row inc in first and last st of row. K back. Place marker to indicate outer foot. Repeat these 2 rows until there are 14 st on needle. K across. On P row inc on last st (inner foot) (15 st). K back. On P row bind off 2 st, P to end of row. K next row. Dec first st beginning next row, P across. K 1 row. Dec first st P row (11 st). K 1 row, P 1 row until piece measures 4 inches. On P row P across, inc 1 st for crotch. Tie thread and pick up stitches from holder. P across.

Body (Stockinette): Inc each end every K row 4 times. Continue K 1 row, P 1 row until body measures 3½ inches from crotch. Dec 1 st each end every K row 4 times. P 1 row, adding 8 st at end of this P row to start arms. K next row, adding 8 st at end of this row. P back, inc 1 st in first and last st. Continuing

72

stockinette, on next 3 K rows, K 2 together each end (arms shaped).

Shoulder: Bind off 5 st at beginning next 4 rows. Bind off first st on next 2 rows. K 1 row (15 st for neck). Start head.

Head: Inc 1 st each end every K row (working in stockinette) 4 times. K 1 row, P 1 row until piece measures 2½ inches from shoulder. Dec each end every K row 4 times (15 st on needle). Bind off 3 st beginning next 4 rows. Then bind off remaining st for top of head.

Repeat these instructions for other side of Gingerbread Boy. Block both pieces. Embroider nose (red), eyes (black) and buttons (white) in satin stitch. Embroider mouth in outline stitch. Sew together on wrong side, leaving open at crotch. Turn right side out. Stuff. Make body rather thick but flat as a real gingerbread boy would be. Close opening. Using white yarn, embroider in outline stitch about ¼" from seam (in front) to simulate icing and across head for "hat."

Treat the Birds

Befriend the birds with this easily constructed bird feeder. Made to hold day-old doughnuts, the bird feeder can hang outside a window; from there you will be able to watch the birds enjoy the treat. A yellow-bellied sapsucker is shown perched on the feeder. The titmouse, chickadee, many woodpeckers, and even the summer tanager will also enjoy the feeder.

MATERIALS:
**lid from a peanut butter or
  mayonnaise jar
nail
woodscrew
8" (½"-diameter) wooden dowel
screw eye
wire to make a hook
day-old doughnuts**

With the nail, make a hole in center of jar lid; place a woodscrew through hole and into one end of wooden dowel. Place a small screw eye in top of wooden dowel.

Place day-old doughnuts (they are cheaper and do not fall apart as easily as fresh ones do) over the dowel.

With a piece of wire, shape a hanger that will slip into the screw eye of feeder and over a tree limb; the feeder should hang far enough below the limb so cats and squirrels cannot reach it.

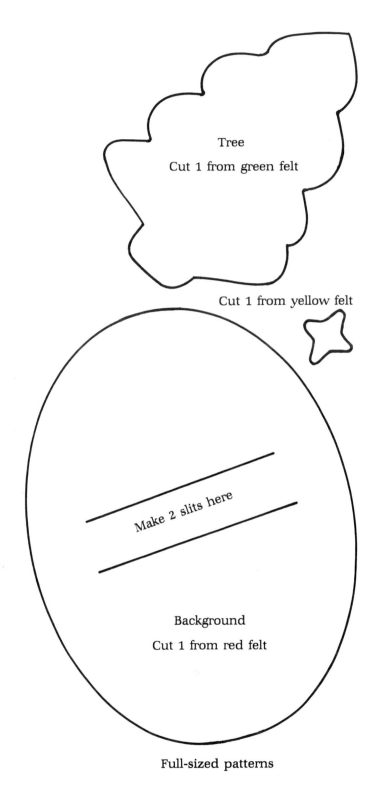

Tree

Cut 1 from green felt

Cut 1 from yellow felt

Make 2 slits here

Background

Cut 1 from red felt

Full-sized patterns

Snip & Glue

Felt is a favorite material for children. It is so easy to cut and glue, and it is a welcome change from the paper that is more often given to children.

Encourage children to help with the holiday preparations by making napkin rings for the family's Christmas breakfast. Felt trees can be ornaments for a child's tree or a gift for a friend—and one could add the child's personal touch as a package decoration on a gift for teacher or grandmother.

For different napkin rings or ornaments, make felt Santas (page 153) and place them on a base of green felt.

TREE NAPKIN RING

MATERIALS (for one napkin ring):
    pattern at left
    4″ × 5″ red felt
    3″ × 4″ green felt
    small scrap yellow felt
    white household glue
    sequins, beads, braid

Trace pattern for red background and cut out to make a paper pattern. Trace around pattern on red felt and cut out felt. Cut the two slits in red felt.

Make a pattern for tree and cut a tree from green felt. Glue tree to red felt above and below two slits; do *not* glue tree to felt between slits.

Cut stars and balls from felt, and glue on tree. Add sequins, beads, and braid for other trims. Allow glue to dry.

Turn napkin ring face down. Lift red felt strip made by the two slits. Fold napkin and slip beneath strip.

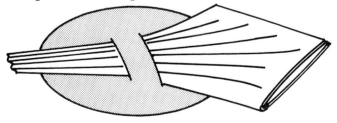

FELT TREE ORNAMENTS

MATERIALS (for one ornament):
  pattern below
  3½" square red felt
  3½" square white felt
  red and green fine-tip pens
  6" gold thread
  white household glue

Trace around the large tree shape to make a pattern. Cut out pattern and draw around it on red felt. Cut out red felt tree.

Make a pattern for white felt tree, trace around pattern on white felt, and cut out. Make a pattern and cut 3 red hearts.

Glue white tree on red tree. Glue red hearts on white tree, with smallest heart at top and largest at bottom.

Draw swirls with a green pen and make a row of dots with a red pen.

Thread gold thread through a needle with a large eye and pull thread through top of tree. Tie in a loop to make a hanger for the ornament.

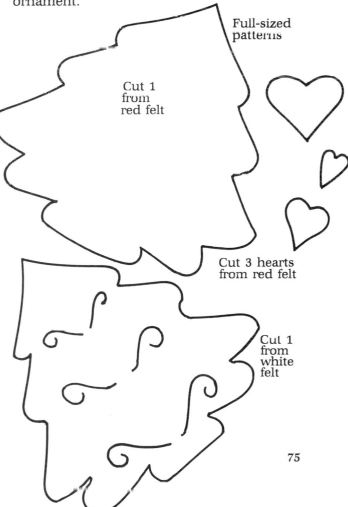

Full-sized patterns

Cut 1 from red felt

Cut 3 hearts from red felt

Cut 1 from white felt

Christmas Geese

Paint a gaggle of geese on a box that never turns its back on anyone. Filled with rolls or a houseplant, the box is a perfect center for a dining table or coffee table. The four geese are cut from wood with a jigsaw or band saw and painted with simple techniques and a minimum of shading.

MATERIALS:
    pattern on page 141
    32" (1" × 8") pine (#2 or better grade)
    4 (1½" × 7½") strips lath or ¼" plywood
    sandpaper
    small, slender nails
    acrylic paint in white, black, green, red, brown, gold
    spray acrylic varnish
    wood glue

Transfer pattern to wood and cut 4 pieces, using a band saw or jigsaw; sand. Transfer features for painting: full goose on nest on outside of pieces and goose head and wreath on inside. Spray a thin coat of varnish over all surfaces to seal the wood; allow to dry. Paint pieces (including lath or plywood for bottom) white; allow to dry.

Paint black beak on inside and outside of goose; extend black across top of beak. Paint eyes black. Using an old brush, stipple green wreath by pouncing up and down with brush (base of bright green with stippling of darker green). Continue wreath over top of goose. After paint has dried, add dots of red for berries. Paint red bow. Paint straw in shades of dark brown to gold. Mix gray from black and white, and add water for a light wash; brush along top of body and head. Add gray wash to define wing and body.

Assemble box by butting end of piece with head of goose against inside of piece with back of goose. Glue and nail sides together. Nail a strip of lath or plywood along two sides of box, with edges even. Space remaining strips evenly between; nail in place. Countersink nails and paint over them. Touch up as needed. Spray with a final coat of varnish.

Line with a Christmas napkin or a dish to hold food.

This wooden box will hold eggs on your kitchen counter, a plant in the family room, or rolls for the breakfast table.

How Many Days?

For a child who enjoys the anticipation of Christmas almost as much as the day itself, begin December with a cross-stitched reindeer that tops a series of pockets—one for each of twenty-four days till Christmas.

MATERIALS:
> **chart on page 152**
> **8″ × 9″ (#14) Aida cloth**
> **embroidery floss in black, white, red, pink, dark pink, green, golden yellow, medium brown, light brown (DMC colors given in color key)**
> **1 yard red fabric**
> **½ yard fusible interfacing**
> **1 yard wide green rickrack**
> **bellpull hardware**

Work design on Aida cloth, filling in colors as shown on the color key.

Cut red fabric front (6½″ × 28″). Stitch Aida to top of fabric. Turn under bottom of Aida; stitch. Cut 3½″ × 6½″ piece of red fabric; place at top of Aida, right side down, and sew. Turn up small piece and sew rickrack at top and bottom of Aida.

Cut 12 (3″ × 6½″) strips of red fabric. Turn under one long side ½″; press and topstitch along edge. Turn under other long side ½″ and press. Place first strip just beneath lower row of rickrack, with topstitched edge at top. Topstitch along bottom edge of strip. Place next strip just beneath first, and sew in place. Add remaining strips.

Cut a back of red fabric and of fusible interfacing to fit front you have made. Fuse interfacing to back. With right sides together, sew back to front except for bottom. Turn and press. Machine stitch through all thicknesses down center front from just beneath lower row of rickrack to bottom of red fabric. Turn down red fabric at top and sew, making a casing for bellpull hardware. Make a casing at bottom. Insert hardware at top and bottom.

For coverlet, cut 1 (4") square of print, 1 from muslin, and 1 from batting. Place muslin on batting; place print, right side down, on muslin. Sew around sides, leaving an opening. Clip corners, turn, and whipstitch. Make bed as directed for coverlet, using 2 (4" × 4¾") pieces of muslin and 1 batting. In same way, make pillow with 2 (1¾" × 4") pieces red fabric and 1 batting. Tack to top of bed. For doll, cut 2 circles of muslin; place together and sew around circle, leaving an opening. Turn, stuff, and whipstitch. Embroider black eyes and eyebrows and a pink mouth. For hair, cut 1½" × 3½" piece of paper. Wrap yarn around shortest dimension to cover 3". Sew twice lengthwise down center of yarn-wrapped paper. Pull paper away from sides of seam and remove; tack "hair" around seam at top of head. Tack head to pillow. Place coverlet on bed, overlapping chin slightly.

Thread needle with heavy thread, and tack coverlet to bed at four corners, leaving ends of thread about ½" long. Make a loop for hanging from same heavy thread.

Sailing Boats & Napping Dolls

'Tis the season for dreaming of ships that come sailing in on Christmas day and dolls with their own visions of sugarplums. With nothing to break and no hard edges, these ornaments are safe enough for young children to hang on a tree or carry in a pocket.

NAPPING DOLL

MATERIALS:
 pattern on page 137
 4" square small print fabric
 ¼ yard unbleached muslin
 10" × 5" batting
 2" × 4" red or polka-dotted fabric
 polyester stuffing
 pink and black embroidery floss
 about 2 yards yellow yarn for hair

SAILING BOAT

MATERIALS:
 pattern on page 137
 12" × 6" white fabric
 6" square quilt batting
 red felt for flag
 3" × 12" navy blue fabric
 polyester stuffing
 heavy cord for hanger

Cut sail (2 pieces) from white fabric. Place pieces, right sides together, on top of batting. Sew around sail except for opening. Trim batting close to seam. Turn, press, and whipstitch opening. Cut flag from red felt and place at top of sail. Machine stitch down center of sail, catching flag as you sew. Cut boat (2 pieces) from navy and sew, right sides together, leaving small opening. Trim corners, turn, and stuff firmly. Whipstitch. Tack sail to boat and add a loop for hanging.

That Extra Flourish

Start now. Make the containers well ahead of the baking rush. You will need a casserole cover for the buffet you are planning—and another for a gift. A wine bag is a pretty gift wrap and a practical substitute for a napkin around a bottle. The Terrific Teddy lid for a cookie jar will cheer up your kitchen and brighten faces with an extra smile. Sew several of the easy-to-make bags and have them ready to hold fresh-from-the-oven treats. You may also want to use the Santa faces as package decorations or make some bags with felt trees (page 75) instead of Santas.

WINE BAGS

Wine bags can be made of quilted or plain fabrics in solid colors or prints. You may find it easier to make bags in assembly-line fashion: cutting first, then hemming tops, and finally sewing seams.

MATERIALS:
   16″ × 17″ quilted fabric
   thread to match
   18″ ribbon (optional)

Make a hem along one 16″ side of fabric. Fold in half with hem at top. Make a French seam down side and across bottom of bag. On inside of bag, fold from a corner so side seam rests atop bottom seam. Measure from corner along side seam 1½″. Sew across this point. (Figure 1.) Turn. The ribbon can be tied around the wine bag when it is filled.

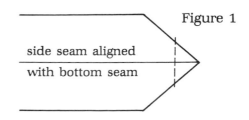

Figure 1

side seam aligned
with bottom seam

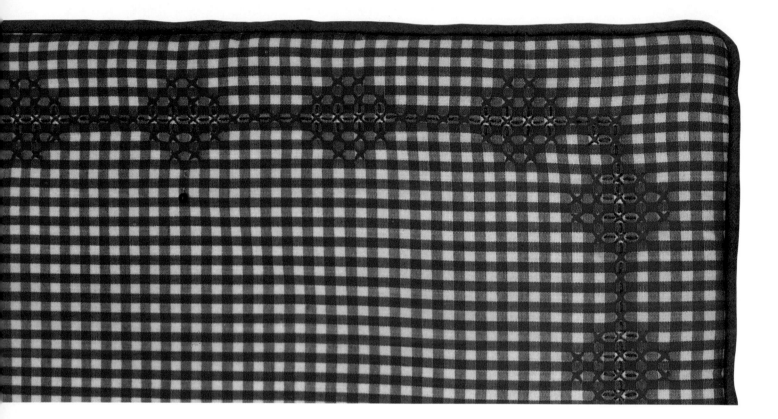

CASEROLE COVER

Carry hot casseroles in style, or fill dish with cookies for a holiday gift. Gingham is the basis for the easy design worked in two stitches—cross-stitch and straight stitch—and two colors—red and green. If you examine gingham closely, you will see that the "squares" are really rectangles and longer in one direction than the other. Since an 8"-square casserole dish has handles on two sides, the cover must also be a rectangle. As you work the design on the gingham, you will notice that the tiny differences in dimensions of individual "squares" are just right for your project. With the same number of stitches on each of the four sides, two sides will be just enough longer to accommodate the handles of the casserole. The finished cover will be a rectangle (13" × 14" plus ½" seam allowances), but begin by cutting a 16" square of gingham. The stitches will do the exact measuring for you.

MATERIALS (8"-square casserole):
  16" square red (¼") gingham
  1 skein red embroidery floss
  1 skein green embroidery floss
  ½ yard green cotton-polyester fabric
  2 yards cord for piping
  15" × 16" batting
  2 yards (¼"-wide) red grosgrain
    ribbon

The photograph above serves as a chart. Half the design is shown; the straight pin marks the center of one side. Begin corner stitch on a *white* square 2" from sides of fabric square. Work one side; turn fabric and work other sides. Trim fabric to an equal amount of fabric beyond design on all sides.

Machine baste batting to wrong side of gingham (½" seams). Cut 15" × 16" green fabric for backing. Cover cord with (1"-wide) bias strip of green to make cording. Cut 8 (9"-long) pieces of ribbon. On right side of gingham, pin ribbon along seam lines,

80

spaced 3″ from corners. Baste. Pin loose ends of ribbon out of the way in center area so they will not be caught in seams.

On right side of gingham, place piping along seam line, raw edges to outside. Stitch. Place backing, right side down, over gingham; sew around sides, except an opening for turning. Turn, press, and whipstich. Tie bows to shape the cover.

TERRIFIC TEDDY

Make the jar as appealing as the cookies inside. Fill a glass cookie jar with your best cookies, tie a gay plaid bow around the neck of the jar, and top with this dashing dressed-to-the-nines holiday bear painted on a wooden plaque.

MATERIALS:
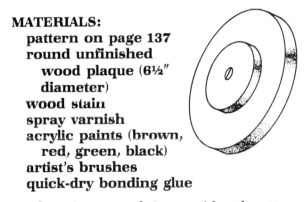
  pattern on page 137
  round unfinished
    wood plaque (6½″
    diameter)
  wood stain
  spray varnish
  acrylic paints (brown,
    red, green, black)
  artist's brushes
  quick-dry bonding glue

Apply stain to wood. Spray with at least two coats of varnish, following manufacturer's instructions, and allow to dry. Transfer pattern to lid, using transfer paper or else bearing down with a dull pencil to make slight indentations in wood. Fill in with acrylic paint, beginning with brown, then adding red and green, and finally adding details with black paint on a tiny brush. Allow to dry overnight; apply a finish coat of varnish.

Attach plaque to original lid of jar. If lid is metal, wood, or cork, apply a strong bonding glue to one surface, press together, and allow to dry. If you do not have the lid, cut another round of wood sized to fit your jar and attach with glue and a screw to underside of plaque (as shown).

SANTA BAGS

Keep extras of these bags on hand to "wrap" gifts for small children or for their teachers. Place a very practical gift for an elderly person in a lighthearted Santa bag.

MATERIALS (for one 7″ bag):
  Santa pattern on page 153
  20″ × 14″ fabric in your choice of
    color and design
  thread to match
  ⅔ yard (¼″-wide) grosgrain ribbon
  small amounts white, red, pink,
    bright pink, and black felt
  white household glue

Cut fabric to size (20″ × 14″), and fold right sides together to a double thickness that measures 20″ × 7″. Sew around raw edges, following the diagram and leaving an opening near one end. (Figure 1.) Do not turn.

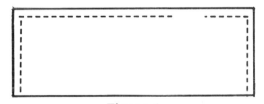

Figure 1

At each of four corners, fold from corner with long side seam lying atop end seam. Measure along seam from corner 1½″. Sew. (See diagram with Wine Bags, page 79.) Clip corners to a ⅜″ seam allowance.

Turn right side out through opening. Turn the half of the bag with the opening inside the other half of the bag, forming a bag with lining. Press, leaving the edges uncreased as shown in the solid green bag or creasing paper-bag fashion as shown in the printed bag. Add loops of ribbon from the sides or from front and back like shopping-bag handles.

For Santa, cut white head, red cap, black glove, pink face, and bright pink nose and mouth. Glue head to hat, overlapping slightly; add other features. Glue or sew Santa to bag or package.

As Tiny as a Walnut

Miniature scenes and ornaments are made from walnuts and bread dough. Santa's sleigh, an angel, a mouse, a basket of gifts and another of flowers are shown here—but the vignettes you make are limited only by your imagination. You may want to place these small one-of-a-kind ornaments beside plates as take-home gifts for your guests.

MATERIALS:
large English walnuts
bread dough (3 slices white bread, 3
   tablespoons white household glue,
   3 drops glycerin, 3 drops lemon
   juice, 3 drops acrylic paint)
acrylic paints
acrylic polymer varnish
drinking straw
toothpicks
small hobby saw or hobby motor
   tool with radial saw attachment

Remove crusts from bread and flake into small crumbs. Add glue, glycerin, and lemon juice; mix well to form a soft ball. Divide dough in 3 parts and tint each part with a drop of red, green, or white acrylic paint. Store bread dough in small plastic bags until ready to use.

For ornaments with closed backs, make bottom cut in walnut from side to side; then cut along seam to bottom cut. Remove shell and nutmeats and clean inside rough edges. For open basket cuts, make 2 similar cuts, leaving a section for handle. Fill bottom of shell with dough and add figures shaped from round and oval balls of dough; use a paint brush and diluted glue to join parts of figures. Make facial features by indenting dough with a toothpick. Add tiny balls of dough for nose, eyes, and ears. Flatten a ball for mouse ears or a teardrop for angel wings.

Make holly leaves and poinsettia petals by flattening a small ball of dough, then cutting around edges with a drinking straw. Use a sharp tool to indent veins of leaves.

Santa's sleigh is carved from popsicle sticks. Carve runners with a sharp hobby knife; use short pieces to make front of sleigh. Glue walnut half to wood frame.

Walnuts may be hung by attaching a metallic cord, or, with the addition of a ball of dough and leaves as a base, they may be sit-up ornaments for a tabletop; attach leaves to shell with a touch of glue. Add tiny round balls for holly berries.

Allow glue to dry thoroughly (about 24 hours). Paint in bright colors with acrylic paints. Seal the ornament with two coats of acrylic polymer varnish so moisture cannot reach the dough.

Celebrations from the Kitchen

Add Southern hospitality to Christmas entertaining with an invitation to "Come for Pie and Coffee." With the recipes in this chapter, you can invite a single friend or a houseful of people to taste the luscious Latticed Cranberry Tart, the Key Lime Pie, Peanut Pie, or Pecan Pie. The pies are as pretty as they are delicious; arrange a buffet of beautiful pies for a special party, or serve a single slice from a silver tray.

For another occasion, make the colorful Candy Cane Bread or one of the other special holiday breads. Fried Cinnamon Buns will melt in your mouth. There are recipes for festive punch and hot tea, and a tantalizing candy-store array of confections. Special tips for decorative touches to add to the foods will help to make the food more attractive; the tips are easy as well as effective.

Few things are as attractive—or as tasty—as a chocolate cake, and there are recipes for two: Chocolate Caramel Cake and Milk Chocolate Cake. A special section is devoted to party foods for your Christmas gatherings. Serve Ham Rolls and Miniature Quiches and, with fruit, a Glorious Amaretto Cheese.

A group of recipes for gift ideas will certainly prove useful; everyone enjoys a gift of food, and there are no worries about finding sizes that fit or favorite colors. This year give Jezebel Sauce or Crunchy Granola or Popcorn Cake Delight. A gift of food is always appropriate.

All the recipes have been tested in the SOUTHERN LIVING kitchens, and we are confident that you will find them special enough to add to your own list of traditional family Christmas favorites.

Come for Pie & Coffee

LATTICED CRANBERRY TART

2 cups sugar
¾ cup water
4 cups fresh cranberries
4 egg yolks
2½ tablespoons all-purpose flour
Dash of salt
½ cup chopped pecans
2 tablespoons butter or margarine
½ teaspoon almond extract
Pastry (recipe follows)
1 egg yolk, beaten
1 teaspoon water

Combine first 3 ingredients in a medium saucepan; cook over medium heat 5 to 7 minutes or until cranberry skins pop. Cool slightly.

Beat 4 egg yolks; stir in flour and salt. Gradually stir about one-fourth of cranberry mixture into yolks; add to remaining cranberry mixture, stirring constantly. Cook over medium heat 1 minute or until thickened, stirring frequently. Stir in pecans, butter, and almond extract.

Roll half of pastry to ⅛-inch thickness on a lightly floured surface. Fit pastry into a 12- × 8- × 1-inch tart pan. Pour cranberry mixture into tart shell.

Roll remaining pastry to ⅛-inch thickness. Cut with a fluted pastry wheel into thin strips. Arrange strips over tart in a diagonal lattice design. Roll rolling pin over pastry on pan edges to trim excess pastry from edges. Combine 1 egg yolk and 1 teaspoon water; mix well. Brush pastry lightly with yolk mixture; bake at 400° for 30 to 35 minutes or until browned. Yield: one 12- × 8- × 1-inch tart.

Pastry:

2 cups all-purpose flour
2 tablespoons sugar
¾ teaspoon salt
⅔ cup plus 2 tablespoons shortening
4 to 6 tablespoons cold water

Combine flour, sugar, and salt; cut in shortening with pastry blender until mixture resembles coarse meal. Sprinkle cold water (1 tablespoon at a time) evenly over surface; stir with a fork until all dry ingredients are moistened. Shape dough into a ball, and chill 30 minutes. Yield: enough for one 12- × 8- × 1-inch tart.

Spread your holiday buffet with an assortment of the South's most tantalizing pies and tarts. Front to back: Latticed Cranberry Tart, Banana Pudding Tarts, and Pineapple-Coconut Pie.

Our elegant Latticed Cranberry Tart is simple to make; just follow the easy instructions.

BANANA PUDDING TARTS

  2 small bananas, sliced
10 baked 3-inch tart shells
  1 (8-ounce) carton commercial sour
    cream
  1 cup milk
  1 (3¾-ounce) package vanilla instant
    pudding mix
    Whipped cream (optional)
    Chopped pecans (optional)
    Maraschino cherries with stems
    (optional)

Place 5 or 6 banana slices in each tart shell; set aside.

Combine sour cream and milk; mix well. Add pudding mix; beat 1 minute on medium speed of electric mixer or until thickened. Spoon into tart shells. Garnish with whipped cream, pecans, and cherries, if desired. Yield: 10 tarts.

PINEAPPLE-COCONUT PIE

    Pastry for 10-inch pie
  2 eggs, beaten
  ½ cup sugar
  2 tablespoons all-purpose flour
  1 cup light corn syrup
  2 tablespoons butter or margarine
  2 tablespoons lemon juice
  1 teaspoon vanilla extract
  1 (8-ounce) can crushed pineapple,
    drained
  ½ cup flaked coconut
  1 egg
  1 teaspoon water

Roll out three-fourths of pastry to ⅛-inch thickness; fit into an 8-inch pieplate. Trim edges even with pieplate. Roll out remaining dough to ⅛-inch thickness; cut into 1-inch circles and arrange around edges of pastry.

Combine 2 eggs, sugar, and flour; beat 1 minute on medium speed of electric mixer or until smooth. Add syrup, butter, lemon juice, and vanilla; beat 1 minute. Stir in pineapple and coconut; pour into pastry shell. Combine 1 egg and water; mix well. Brush over pastry; bake at 400° for 15 minutes. Reduce heat to 350°, and bake an additional 25 minutes or until set. Yield: one 8-inch pie.

Try this top-notch finish for holiday pie baking. Using enough pastry for a 10-inch pie, roll out three-fourths of pastry and fit into an 8- or 9-inch pieplate. Trim pastry edges even with the pieplate. Roll out the extra dough and cut into 1-inch circles. Overlap the circles around the edge of pastry. Then bake according to the recipe directions.

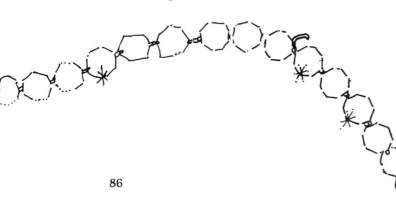

BASIC PASTRY

1½ cups all-purpose flour
½ teaspoon salt
½ cup shortening
3 to 5 tablespoons cold water

Combine flour and salt; cut in shortening with a pastry blender until mixture resembles coarse meal. Sprinkle cold water (1 tablespoon at a time) evenly over surface; stir with a fork until all dry ingredients are moistened. Shape dough into a ball.

Roll out dough to ⅛-inch thickness on a lightly floured surface. Place in a 9-inch pieplate; trim off excess pastry around edges. Fold edges under and flute. Fill shell with desired filling and bake as the recipe directs.

For a baked pastry shell, prick bottom and sides of shell with a fork. Bake at 425° for 12 to 15 minutes or until golden brown. Yield: one 9-inch shell.

FRENCH APPLE PIE

Pastry for double-crust 9-inch pie
6 cups peeled, thinly sliced cooking apples
1½ cups sugar
½ teaspoon ground cinnamon
½ teaspoon ground nutmeg
3 tablespoons cornstarch
Grated rind of 1 lemon
Juice of 1 lemon
¼ cup raisins
3 tablespoons butter or margarine

Line a 9-inch pieplate with half of pastry; set aside.

Combine remaining ingredients, except butter, mixing well. Spoon filling into pastry

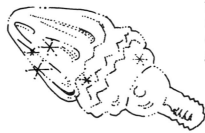

shell, and dot with butter. Cover with top crust, and slit in several places to allow steam to escape; seal and flute edges. Bake at 400° for 15 minutes; reduce heat to 350°, and bake an additional 40 minutes. Yield: one 9-inch pie.

OLD-FASHIONED LEMON MERINGUE PIE

1 cup sugar
3 tablespoons cornstarch
¼ teaspoon salt
2 cups milk
3 eggs, separated
1 teaspoon grated lemon rind
⅓ cup lemon juice
3 tablespoons butter or margarine
1 baked 9-inch pastry shell
¼ teaspoon cream of tartar
¼ cup plus 2 tablespoons sugar
½ teaspoon vanilla extract

Combine 1 cup sugar, cornstarch, and salt in a heavy saucepan. Gradually add milk, stirring until blended. Cook over medium heat, stirring constantly, until mixture thickens and comes to a boil. Boil 1 minute, stirring constantly. Remove from heat.

Beat egg yolks until thick and lemon colored. Gradually stir about one-fourth of hot mixture into yolks; add to remaining hot mixture, stirring constantly. Cook over medium heat, stirring constantly, for 2 to 3 minutes. Remove from heat; stir in lemon rind, lemon juice, and butter. Pour into pastry shell.

Beat egg whites (at room temperature) and cream of tartar until foamy. Gradually add remaining sugar, 1 tablespoon at a time, beating until stiff peaks form; beat in vanilla. Spread meringue over filling, sealing to edge of pastry. Bake at 400° for 10 minutes or until golden brown. Yield: one 9-inch pie.

Slice into luscious Lime Party Pie for a light, refreshing dessert.

LIME PARTY PIE

    1 envelope unflavored gelatin
    ¼ cup cold water
    4 eggs, separated
    ½ cup sugar
  1½ teaspoons grated lime rind
    ½ cup fresh lime juice
    ½ cup sugar
    ½ cup whipping cream, whipped
    1 baked 9-inch pastry shell
      Lime slices

Soften gelatin in water, and set mixture aside.

Combine egg yolks, ½ cup sugar, lime rind and juice in top of double boiler; beat well. Cook over boiling water, stirring constantly, until thick and smooth (about 15 minutes). Stir in gelatin, and cool.

Beat egg whites (at room temperature) until foamy. Gradually add ½ cup sugar, 1 tablespoon at a time, beating until stiff peaks form.

Fold egg whites and whipped cream into cooked mixture, and spoon into pastry shell. Chill pie several hours or until filling is set. Garnish with lime slices. Yield: one 9-inch pie.

CHOCOLATE CREAM PIE

    2 (1-ounce) squares unsweetened
        chocolate
    1 cup sugar
    ¼ cup all-purpose flour
    ½ teaspoon salt
    2 cups milk
    4 eggs, separated
    2 tablespoons butter or margarine
    2 teaspoons vanilla extract
    1 baked 9-inch pastry shell
    ½ cup sugar

Melt chocolate over low heat in a heavy saucepan; cool.

Combine 1 cup sugar, flour, and salt in a heavy saucepan; mix well. Stir in milk and chocolate; bring to a boil, and boil 1 minute, stirring constantly. Beat egg yolks. Gradually stir about one-fourth of hot mixture into yolks; add to remaining hot mixture, stirring constantly. Return to a boil and boil 1 minute, stirring constantly. Add butter and vanilla; stir until butter melts. Pour into pastry shell; set aside.

Beat egg whites (at room temperature) until foamy. Gradually add ½ cup sugar, 1 tablespoon at a time, beating until stiff peaks form. Spread meringue over filling, sealing to edge of pastry. Bake at 400° for 10 minutes or until golden brown. Let pie cool before serving. Yield: one 9-inch pie.

SOUTHERN PEANUT PIE

    3 eggs, well beaten
    1 cup dark corn syrup
    ½ cup firmly packed dark brown
         sugar
    ⅓ cup peanut butter
    1 teaspoon vanilla extract
    ⅛ teaspoon salt
    1 cup dry roasted, salted peanuts
    1 unbaked 9-inch pastry shell

Combine first 6 ingredients; mix well. Stir in peanuts; pour into pastry shell. Bake at 400° for 12 minutes; reduce heat to 350°, and bake an additional 30 to 35 minutes or until set. Yield: one 9-inch pie.

BRANDY PECAN PIE

    2 eggs, beaten
    ½ cup half-and-half
    ¾ cup sugar
    2 tablespoons all-purpose flour
    ½ teaspoon salt
    1 tablespoon molasses
    1 cup light corn syrup
    1 teaspoon vanilla extract
 1½ tablespoons brandy
    1 cup coarsely chopped pecans
    1 unbaked 9-inch pastry shell

Combine eggs and half-and-half; beat well. Add next 6 ingredients, and mix well. Stir in brandy and pecans. Pour into pastry shell; bake at 350° for 40 to 50 minutes or until set. Yield: one 9-inch pie.

SWEET POTATO CREAM PIE IN GINGERSNAP CRUST

    ¾ cup evaporated milk
    ¾ cup water
 1½ cups cooked, mashed sweet
         potatoes
    ½ cup dark corn syrup
    ⅓ cup sugar
    3 tablespoons cornstarch
    1 teaspoon ground cinnamon
    ¾ teaspoon ground ginger
    ½ teaspoon salt
    2 eggs, well beaten
    ½ teaspoon vanilla extract
    3 tablespoons butter or margarine
       Gingersnap crust (recipe follows)
       Sweetened whipped cream
         (optional)
       Chopped pecans (optional)

Combine milk and water in a large saucepan; scald. Add sweet potatoes and corn syrup; mix well. Combine sugar, cornstarch, cinnamon, ginger, and salt; mix well. Gradually add sugar mixture to milk mixture; cook over low heat, stirring constantly until thickened. Gradually stir about one-fourth of hot mixture into eggs; add to remaining hot mixture, stirring constantly.

Cook over low heat 2 minutes, stirring constantly. Remove from heat; add vanilla and butter, stirring until butter melts. Cool slightly; pour into cooled gingersnap crust. Let cool completely. Garnish with whipped cream and pecans, if desired. Yield: one 9-inch pie.

Gingersnap crust:

 1¼ cups gingersnap crumbs
    1 tablespoon sugar
    ¼ cup butter or margarine, softened

Combine all ingredients in a small bowl; blend well. Press firmly into a buttered 9-inch pieplate. Bake at 375° for 6 to 8 minutes. Cool. Yield: one 9-inch pie crust.

Beverages

WASSAIL

- 2 (32-ounce) bottles cranberry juice cocktail
- 3 (12-ounce) cans frozen orange juice concentrate, thawed and undiluted
- 4½ cups water
- 3 tablespoons sugar
- 2 teaspoons ground cinnamon
- 1 (25.4-ounce) bottle Sauterne
  Orange slices (optional)
  Whole cloves (optional)

Combine first 5 ingredients in a large Dutch oven; simmer 30 minutes. Stir in Sauterne. Pour wassail into a heat-proof punch bowl. Float clove-studded orange slices in punch, if desired. Yield: 5 quarts.

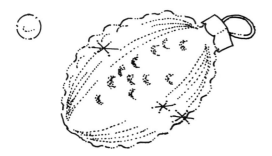

CHOCOLATE ALEXANDERS

- 1 quart skim milk
- 2 tablespoons instant coffee powder
- ¼ cup chocolate syrup
- ½ teaspoon vanilla extract
- ½ to 1 teaspoon brandy extract
  Frozen whipped topping, thawed
  Grated chocolate (optional)

Combine first 3 ingredients in a heavy saucepan; cook over medium heat, stirring frequently, until hot. Stir in flavorings. Ladle into mugs, and garnish with whipped topping. Sprinkle with chocolate, if desired. Yield: 1 quart.

PINEAPPLE SPARKLE

- 1½ quarts unsweetened pineapple juice
- 1½ cups orange juice
- ¾ cup lemon juice
- 3 tablespoons lime juice
- 1¼ cups sugar
- 2 (28-ounce) bottles ginger ale, chilled
- 1 (28-ounce) bottle club soda, chilled
  Orange and lime slices (optional)

Combine fruit juice and sugar; stir until sugar dissolves. Cover and chill 3 to 4 hours. To serve, pour chilled mixture over ice in punch bowl; slowly pour in ginger ale and club soda, stirring gently. Garnish with orange and lime slices, if desired. Yield: about 5 quarts.

HOT CRANBERRY TEA

- 4 cups fresh cranberries
- 3½ quarts water
- 12 whole cloves
- 4 (3-inch) sticks cinnamon
  Juice of 2 lemons
  Juice of 2 oranges
- 2 cups sugar

Combine first 4 ingredients in a Dutch oven; bring to a boil. Cover, reduce heat, and simmer 12 minutes. Strain through several thicknesses of cheesecloth, squeezing gently. Add lemon juice, orange juice, and sugar; stir until sugar dissolves. Serve hot. Yield: 3½ quarts.

Warm your guests with a cup of piping Hot Cranberry Tea.

AMARETTO SLUSH

- 1 cup sugar
- 4½ cups water
- 1 (6-ounce) can frozen lemonade concentrate, thawed and undiluted
- 1 (6-ounce) can frozen orange juice concentrate, thawed and undiluted
- 1 cup amaretto
  Lemon-lime carbonated beverage, chilled
  Maraschino cherries (optional)

Combine sugar and water in a saucepan, stirring well. Bring to a boil, stirring until sugar dissolves. Reduce heat; simmer 15 minutes. Combine sugar mixture and next 3 ingredients; stir well. Freeze mixture overnight.

Break frozen mixture into chunks. Scoop into glasses, filling one-third to one-half full. Add carbonated beverage; stir until slushy. Top each serving with a cherry, if desired. Yield: 7½ cups.

PINEAPPLE EGGNOG

- 1 (46-ounce) can pineapple juice
- 2 cups whipping cream
- 8 eggs, separated
- 1 cup sugar, divided

Place pineapple juice in a small Dutch oven; bring to a boil. Remove from heat; gradually add cream, stirring constantly. Beat egg yolks in a large mixing bowl until thick and lemon colored; gradually add ½ cup sugar, beating well. Gradually stir about one-fourth of hot pineapple mixture into yolks; add to remaining hot mixture, stirring constantly. Cover and chill at least 1 hour.

Beat egg whites (at room temperature) until foamy. Gradually add remaining sugar, 1 tablespoon at a time, beating until stiff peaks form. Fold into pineapple mixture. Yield: about 3 quarts.

SOUTHERN HIGHBALL

- ½ cup plus 1 tablespoon bourbon
- 3 to 4 cups cola carbonated beverage, chilled
- 3 tablespoons maraschino cherry juice
- ½ cup whipping cream, whipped and divided
- ¼ cup plus 2 tablespoons vodka

Combine bourbon, carbonated beverage, cherry juice, and ¼ cup whipped cream; stir well. Stir in vodka; mix well. Serve over ice in highball glasses; top each glass with remaining whipped cream. Yield: 6 to 8 servings.

HOT SPICED APPLE CIDER

- 1 teaspoon whole allspice
- 16 whole cloves
- 2 (3-inch) sticks cinnamon
- 2 quarts apple cider
- ½ cup firmly packed brown sugar
- 1 orange, cut into ½-inch slices

Tie allspice, cloves, and cinnamon in a cheesecloth bag. Combine spice bag, apple cider, sugar, and orange slices in a large saucepan; bring to a boil. Reduce heat and simmer 15 minutes. Remove spice bag; ladle into mugs. Yield: 2 quarts.

HOLIDAY SANGRIA

- 6 oranges, thinly sliced
- 3 lemons, thinly sliced
- 3 limes, thinly sliced
- 1 cup sugar
- 1 cup brandy
- 3 (25.4-ounce) bottles Burgundy or other dry red wine

Place fruit slices in a large punch bowl; sprinkle with sugar. Pour brandy over fruit; cover and let stand at least 1 hour. Add wine; mix well. Let stand at least 30 minutes. Serve over ice. Yield: 3½ quarts.

Breads

PECAN TEA RING

- 2 packages dry yeast
- 2¼ cups warm water (105° to 115°) divided
- ½ cup sugar
- ½ cup butter or margarine, melted
- 2 eggs, beaten
- 2 teaspoons salt
- 7½ to 8 cups all-purpose flour, divided
- ¼ cup butter or margarine, divided and softened
- 1 cup finely chopped pecans
- ½ cup sugar
- 2 tablespoons ground cinnamon
- 1 egg white
- 1 tablespoon water
- 2 cups sifted powdered sugar
- 3 tablespoons milk
- 1 teaspoon vegetable oil
- 2 teaspoons vanilla extract
  Chopped candied cherries
  Additional chopped pecans

Dissolve yeast in ½ cup warm water in a large bowl; let stand 5 minutes. Add remaining warm water, ½ cup sugar, ½ cup butter, eggs, salt, and 2 cups flour; beat at low speed of electric mixer for 2 minutes. Stir in enough remaining flour to make a soft dough; cover and let rest 10 minutes.

Turn dough out on a lightly floured surface, and knead until smooth and elastic (8 to 10 minutes). Place dough in a well-greased bowl, turning to grease top. Cover and let rise in a warm place, free from drafts, 1 hour or until doubled in bulk.

Punch dough down; divide in half. Roll each half into a 15- × 9-inch rectangle. Spread each with 2 tablespoons butter, leaving a 1-inch margin. Combine 1 cup pecans, ½ cup sugar, and cinnamon; mix well and sprinkle half over each rectangle, leaving a 1-inch margin.

Roll up dough, jellyroll fashion, beginning at a long side; pinch edges to seal. Place each roll on a large, greased baking sheet, seam side down; shape into a ring and pinch ends together to seal.

Using kitchen shears, make cuts in dough every 2 inches around rings, cutting two-thirds of the way through roll at each cut. Gently turn each piece of dough on its side, slightly overlapping slices. Combine egg white and 1 tablespoon water; beat well. Brush over dough; cover and let rise in a warm place, free from drafts, 45 minutes or until doubled in bulk. Bake at 375° for 20 to 25 minutes or until golden brown; transfer to wire racks. Combine powdered sugar, milk, oil, and vanilla; stir until smooth. Drizzle over bread while warm; garnish with candied cherries and additional chopped pecans. Yield: 2 coffee cakes.

FUNNEL CAKES

- 1¼ cups all-purpose flour
- 1 teaspoon baking soda
- ¾ teaspoon baking powder
- ¼ teaspoon salt
- 2 tablespoons sugar
- 1 egg, beaten
- ¾ cup milk
  Vegetable oil
  Sifted powdered sugar

Combine first 7 ingredients in a bowl, beating until smooth. Heat ¼ inch oil to 375° in a skillet. Cover bottom opening of a funnel with finger. (Funnel with a ⅜-inch opening works best.) Pour ¼ cup batter into funnel. Hold funnel over skillet. Remove finger from funnel end to release batter into hot oil; move funnel in a slow, circular motion to form a spiral.

Fry each funnel cake 1 minute or until edges are golden brown; turn and fry until golden. Drain on absorbent paper towels. Repeat with remaining batter. Sprinkle with powdered sugar; serve warm. Yield: about 8 (5-inch) cakes.

FRIED CINNAMON BUNS

- ¾ cup milk
- ¼ cup sugar
- 1 teaspoon salt
- ¼ cup butter or margarine
- 1 package dry yeast
- ¼ cup warm water (105° to 115°)
- 1 egg, beaten
- 3 to 3½ cups all-purpose flour
- ¾ cup sugar
- 1 teaspoon ground cinnamon
  Vegetable oil
- 1½ cups sifted powdered sugar
- 2 tablespoons water

Scald milk; add sugar, salt, and butter, stirring until butter melts. Cool to 105° to 115°.

Dissolve yeast in warm water in a large bowl; let stand 5 minutes. Add milk mixture, egg, and 1½ cups flour. Beat at medium speed of electric mixer until smooth. Gradually stir in enough of remaining flour to make a stiff dough.

Turn dough out on a lightly floured surface, and knead until smooth and elastic (about 8 to 10 minutes). Place dough in a well-greased bowl, turning to grease top. Cover and let rise in a warm place, free from drafts, 1 hour or until doubled in bulk.

Punch dough down; divide in half. Roll each half into a 14- × 9-inch rectangle. Combine ¾ cup sugar and cinnamon; mix well. Sprinkle half of sugar mixture over each rectangle. Carefully roll up jellyroll fashion, beginning at short side; firmly pinch edges and ends to seal. Cut each roll into 1-inch slices. Place slices 2 inches apart on greased baking sheets; flatten each bun using the bottom of a glass or an egg turner. Cover and let rise in a warm place, free from drafts, 45 minutes or until doubled in bulk.

Heat 2 inches of oil to 375° in a skillet. Fry buns for 1 minute or until golden brown; turn and fry until golden. Drain buns on a tea towel. Combine powdered sugar and water; stir until smooth. Drizzle over warm buns. Yield: ½ dozen.

This year, choose from our selection of holiday breads. Clockwise from front: Finnish Coffee Bread, Fried Cinnamon Buns, Molasses Round Bread, and Raisin English Muffins.

FINNISH COFFEE BREAD

- 1½ cups milk
- 1½ cups sugar
- 2 teaspoons salt
- 1 cup butter or margarine
- 1 tablespoon plus 1 teaspoon ground cardamom
- 3 envelopes dry yeast
- 1⅓ cups warm water (105° to 115°)
- 5 eggs, beaten
- 10 cups all-purpose flour, divided
- 1 egg
- 2 tablespoons water
  Sugar

Scald milk. Add sugar, salt, butter, and cardamom; stir until butter melts. Cool to 105° to 115°. Dissolve yeast in warm water in large bowl; let stand 5 minutes. Add milk mixture, 5 eggs, and 2 cups flour. Beat at medium speed of electric mixer until smooth. Stir in enough remaining flour to make soft dough (mixture will be sticky).

Turn dough out on a heavily floured surface and knead until smooth and elastic (about 8 to 10 minutes). Place dough in a well-greased bowl, turning to grease top. Cover and let rise in a warm place, free from drafts, 2 hours or until doubled in bulk.

Grease 4 (9-inch) cakepans; set aside. Punch dough down; divide dough into four portions. Divide each portion into thirds; shape each third into a 14-inch rope (total of 12 ropes). Place 3 ropes side by side (do not stretch); pinch ends together at one end to seal. Braid ropes; pinch ends to seal. Carefully transfer each braid to a prepared pan; starting with one end of braid in center of pan, twist braid around to fit pan.

Cover and let rise in a warm place, free from drafts, 50 to 60 minutes or until doubled in bulk. Bake at 350° for 20 minutes or until bread sounds hollow when tapped. Combine 1 egg and 2 tablespoons water; beat well. Brush over warm loaves; sprinkle with sugar. Yield: 4 loaves.

Note: The loaves may be left as braids and baked on cookie sheets.

RAISIN ENGLISH MUFFINS

1 package dry yeast
1 cup warm water (105° to 115°)
1 cup milk
2 tablespoons sugar
1 teaspoon salt
3 tablespoons butter or margarine, softened
5 to 5½ cups all-purpose flour
1 cup raisins
   Cornmeal

Dissolve yeast in water in a large mixing bowl; let stand 5 minutes.

Combine milk, sugar, salt, and butter in a small saucepan; stir over medium heat until butter melts. Cool to 105° to 115°.

Stir milk mixture and 3 cups flour into yeast mixture; beat until smooth. Add enough remaining flour to form a stiff dough. Stir in raisins.

Turn dough out on a floured surface, and knead 2 minutes or until dough can be shaped into a ball (dough will be slightly sticky). Place in a well-greased bowl, turning to grease top. Cover and let rise in a warm place (85°), free from drafts, about 1 hour or until doubled in bulk.

Punch dough down, and divide in half. Turn one half out onto a smooth surface heavily sprinkled with cornmeal. Pat dough into a circle, ½-inch thick, using palms of hands; cut into rounds with a 2¾-inch cutter. (Cut carefully as leftover dough should not be reused.)

Sprinkle two baking sheets with cornmeal. Transfer cut dough rounds to baking sheets, placing 2 inches apart with cornmeal side down (one side of dough should remain free of cornmeal). Repeat process with remaining half of dough. Cover and let rise in a warm place (85°), free from drafts, 30 minutes or until doubled in bulk.

Using a wide spatula, transfer rounds to a lightly greased electric skillet preheated to 360°. Place cornmeal side down; cook 6 minutes. Turn muffins and cook an additional 6 minutes. Cool on wire racks. To serve, split muffins and toast until lightly browned. Muffins should be stored in an airtight container. Yield: about 1½ dozen.

Note: Muffins may be cooked over medium-high heat in a skillet.

CANDY CANE BREAD

1½ cups chopped dried apricots
2 cups boiling water
2 packages dry yeast
½ cup warm water (105° to 115°)
2 cups commercial sour cream
¼ cup plus 2 tablespoons sugar
¼ cup butter or margarine
1½ teaspoons salt
2 eggs, beaten
6 to 6½ cups unbleached flour, divided
1½ cups chopped maraschino cherries
¼ cup butter or margarine, melted
1 cup sifted powdered sugar
1 tablespoon plus 1 to 2 teaspoons milk
   Chopped candied cherries

Combine apricots and boiling water; cover and let stand 1 hour. Drain well, and set aside.

Dissolve yeast in warm water in a large bowl; let stand 5 minutes. Combine sour cream, sugar, butter, and salt in a heavy saucepan; stir over low heat until butter melts. Cool to 105° to 115°.

Add sour cream mixture, eggs, and 2 cups flour to yeast mixture. Beat at low speed of electric mixer until smooth. Stir in enough of remaining flour to make a soft dough.

Turn dough out on a floured surface and knead until smooth and elastic (about 8 to 10 minutes). Place dough in a well-greased

Our apricot- and cherry-filled Candy Cane Bread delights children of any age.

bowl, turning to grease top. Cover and let rise in a warm place, free from drafts, 1 hour or until doubled in bulk.

Punch dough down; divide dough into 3 equal portions. Roll each portion into a 15- x 6-inch rectangle on a lightly floured surface; transfer to greased baking sheets. Make 2-inch cuts on both long sides of rectangles ½-inch apart, leaving a 2-inch uncut strip down the center. Combine apricots and cherries; spread down the center of dough rectangles. Alternately criss-cross strips over the fruit; gently stretch dough to 22 inches long. Curve one end to resemble a cane. Bake at 375° for 15 to 20 minutes or until brown. Brush each cane with melted butter; let cool. Combine powdered sugar and milk; stir until smooth, and drizzle over coffee cakes. Garnish with chopped candied cherries. Yield: 3 coffee cakes.

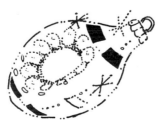

MOLASSES ROUND BREAD

¼ **cup butter or margarine, softened**
½ **cup firmly packed brown sugar**
2 **eggs**
1 **cup applesauce**
¼ **cup molasses**
1¼ **cups all-purpose flour**
1 **cup whole wheat flour**
2 **teaspoons baking powder**
1 **teaspoon baking soda**
½ **teaspoon salt**
½ **cup raisins**

Cream butter; gradually add sugar, beating well. Add eggs, one at a time, beating well after each addition. Add applesauce and molasses; beat until smooth. Combine flour, baking powder, soda, and salt; stir into creamed mixture. Stir in raisins.

Spoon batter into 3 greased and floured 16-ounce vegetable cans; bake at 350° for 35 to 40 minutes or until a wooden pick inserted in center comes out clean. Cool in cans 10 minutes; remove from cans, and cool completely on wire racks. Serve plain or with cream cheese. Yield: 3 loaves.

APRICOT-PECAN BREAD

1 cup all-purpose flour
¾ cup whole wheat flour
2 teaspoons baking powder
½ teaspoon baking soda
½ teaspoon salt
½ cup butter, softened
¾ cup sugar
2 eggs
1 cup mashed banana
¼ cup milk
¾ cup chopped dried apricots
½ cup coarsely chopped pecans

Combine first 5 ingredients; set aside.

Cream butter; gradually add sugar, beating well. Add eggs, one at a time, beating well after each addition.

Combine banana and milk; add to creamed mixture alternately with dry ingredients. Fold in apricots and pecans. Pour batter into a greased and floured 8½- × 4½- × 3-inch loafpan. Bake at 350° for 1 hour or until a wooden pick inserted in center comes out clean. Cool in pan 10 minutes; remove from pan, and let cool completely on a wire rack. Yield: 1 loaf.

GLAZED CRANBERRY-LEMON BREAD

¼ cup butter or margarine, softened
¾ cup sugar
2 eggs
2 teaspoons grated lemon rind
2 cups all-purpose flour
2½ teaspoons baking powder
½ teaspoon salt
¾ cup milk
1 cup fresh cranberries, chopped
½ cup chopped walnuts
2 tablespoons sifted powdered sugar
2 teaspoons lemon juice

Cream butter; gradually add sugar, beating well. Add eggs, one at a time, beating well after each addition. Add lemon rind; mix well. Combine flour, baking powder, and salt; add to creamed mixture alternately with milk, beginning and ending with flour mixture. Mix well after each addition. Stir in cranberries and walnuts.

Pour batter into a greased and floured 9- × 5- × 3-inch loafpan; bake at 350° for 55 to 60 minutes or until a wooden pick inserted in center comes out clean. Cool in pan 10 minutes; remove from pan, and let cool completely.

Combine powdered sugar and lemon juice; mix well and drizzle over bread. Yield: 1 loaf.

CHEESE & PEPPER MUFFINS

3 tablespoons finely chopped green pepper
¼ cup finely chopped onion
1 (2-ounce) jar diced pimiento, drained
¾ cup (3 ounces) shredded sharp Cheddar cheese
2½ cups all-purpose flour
¼ cup yellow cornmeal
2 tablespoons baking powder
1 teaspoon salt
¼ teaspoon red pepper
¼ cup sugar
2 eggs, beaten
1½ cups milk
¼ cup shortening, melted

Combine first 10 ingredients in a medium mixing bowl; make a well in center of mixture. Combine eggs, milk, and shortening; add to dry ingredients, stirring just until moistened. Spoon into greased muffin pans, filling two-thirds full. Bake at 400° for 20 to 25 minutes. Yield: 1½ dozen.

Cakes & Fruitcakes

SPICED PUMPKIN CAKE

1 (18.5-ounce) package yellow cake
    mix without pudding
4 eggs
1 cup canned pumpkin
¾ cup sugar
½ cup vegetable oil
¼ cup water
1 teaspoon ground cinnamon
    Dash of ground nutmeg
1½ cups sifted powdered sugar
1½ to 2 tablespoons milk

Combine first 8 ingredients in a large mixing bowl; beat 2 minutes on medium speed of electric mixer. Pour into a greased and floured 10-inch Bundt pan; bake at 350° for 50 to 55 minutes. Cool in pan 10 minutes; remove from pan. Cool on wire rack.

Combine powdered sugar and milk; stir until smooth. Drizzle over cake. Yield: one 10-inch cake.

RASPBERRY CHEESECAKE

1 cup graham cracker crumbs
2 tablespoons sugar
3 tablespoons butter or margarine,
    melted
4 (8-ounce) packages cream cheese,
    softened
¾ cup sugar
4 eggs
2 egg yolks
¼ cup cognac
1 teaspoon vanilla extract
1 (8-ounce) carton commercial sour
    cream
3 tablespoons sifted powdered sugar
2 to 3 tablespoons cognac
    Raspberry Sauce

Combine first 3 ingredients, mixing well. Firmly press mixture into bottom of a 9-inch springform pan. Bake at 350° for 8 minutes. Cool completely.

Beat cream cheese with electric mixer until light and fluffy; gradually add sugar, mixing well. Add eggs and egg yolks, one at a time, beating well after each addition. Stir in ¼ cup cognac and vanilla; mix well. Pour mixture into prepared pan. Bake at 350° for 10 minutes. Reduce oven temperature to 200°, and bake an additional 50 minutes.

Combine sour cream, powdered sugar, and 2 to 3 tablespoons cognac; carefully spread over hot cheesecake. Bake at 350° for 15 minutes. Let cool to room temperature on a wire rack; chill 8 hours or overnight.

Remove sides of springform pan. Spoon Raspberry Sauce over each serving. Yield: one 9-inch cheesecake.

Raspberry Sauce:
2 (10-ounce) packages frozen
    raspberries, thawed
2 tablespoons cornstarch
¼ cup sugar
¼ cup water
1½ teaspoons orange juice
2 to 3 tablespoons Cointreau or
    other orange-flavored liqueur

Drain raspberries, reserving juice. Press raspberries through a sieve or food mill, discarding seeds; set aside.

Combine raspberry juice and cornstarch in a heavy saucepan; stir until smooth. Add sugar, raspberry pulp, water, and orange juice. Cook over low heat, stirring constantly, until smooth and thickened. Stir in Cointreau. Cool. Yield: about 1⅓ cups.

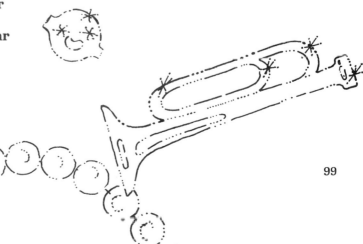

Luscious Sweet Potato Cake with Fresh Coconut Filling makes a delightfully different holiday cake.

SWEET POTATO CAKE WITH FRESH COCONUT FILLING

- 1½ cups sugar
- 1 cup vegetable oil
- 4 eggs, separated
- 2¾ cups sifted cake flour
- 1 tablespoon baking powder
- ¼ teaspoon salt
- 2 teaspoons ground cinnamon
- 1 teaspoon ground ginger
- ½ teaspoon ground cloves
- 1½ cups shredded raw sweet potato
- ¼ cup hot water
- ½ cup chopped walnuts
  Fresh Coconut Filling
  Orange rind bow (optional)

Combine sugar and oil in a large mixing bowl; beat 2 minutes on medium speed of electric mixer. Add egg yolks, one at a time, beating well after each addition.

Combine flour, baking powder, salt, and spices; mix well. Stir flour mixture, sweet potatoes, hot water, and walnuts into creamed mixture. Beat egg whites (at room temperature) until stiff peaks form; fold into batter.

Pour batter into 3 greased and floured 8-inch round cakepans; bake at 350° for 30 to 35 minutes or until a wooden pick inserted in center comes out clean. Cool in pan 10 minutes; remove layers from pans, and let cool completely.

Spread Fresh Coconut Filling between layers and on top of cake. Garnish with an orange rind bow, if desired. Cover and chill 3 to 4 hours. Yield: one 3-layer cake.

Fresh Coconut Filling:

- ½ cup sugar
- ¼ cup cornstarch
- ¼ teaspoon salt
- 2 cups milk
- 2 eggs, beaten
- 1 cup grated fresh coconut
- 1 teaspoon vanilla extract

100

Combine sugar, cornstarch, and salt in a heavy saucepan; gradually stir in milk. Cook, stirring constantly, over medium heat until mixture thickens and boils. Remove from heat. Gradually stir about one-fourth of hot mixture into eggs; add to remaining hot mixture, stirring constantly. Return to a boil and cook for 1 minute, stirring constantly, or until thickened. Remove from heat; stir in coconut and vanilla. Let cool; cover and chill 1 to 2 hours. Yield: enough for one 3-layer cake.

HOLIDAY NUT CAKE

- 2 cups butter, softened
- 2 cups sugar
- 6 eggs
- 2 teaspoons vanilla extract
- 4 cups all-purpose flour, divided
- ½ teaspoon baking powder
- ¼ teaspoon salt
- 1 (8-ounce) package dates, chopped
- ½ pound candied red cherries, chopped
- 4 cups chopped pecans
  Glaze (recipe follows)
  Candied red and green cherries (optional)

Grease a 10-inch tube pan. Line with brown paper and grease well; set aside.

Cream butter; gradually add sugar, beating until light and fluffy. Add eggs, one at a time, beating well after each addition. Stir in vanilla.

Combine 3 cups flour, baking powder, and salt; add to creamed mixture, mixing well. Dredge dates, ½ pound cherries, and pecans in remaining 1 cup flour; stir into batter.

Spoon batter into prepared pan. Bake at 250° for 2 hours and 30 minutes to 2 hours and 45 minutes or until a wooden pick inserted in center comes out clean. Cool in pan 10 minutes; remove from pan, peel paper liner from cake, and cool completely. Drizzle with glaze; garnish with green and red candied cherries, if desired. Yield: one 10-inch cake.

Glaze:

- 2 cups sifted powdered sugar
- 3 tablespoons butter or margarine, softened
- 2 tablespoons plus 1 teaspoon milk
- 2 teaspoons vanilla extract

Combine all ingredients; beat on medium speed of electric mixer until smooth. Yield: about 1½ cups.

BEST BUTTERMILK POUND CAKE

- ½ cup butter or margarine, softened
- ½ cup shortening
- 2¾ cups sugar
- 5 eggs
- 3 cups all-purpose flour
- ½ teaspoon baking soda
- 1 cup buttermilk
- 1 teaspoon vanilla extract

Cream butter and shortening; gradually add sugar, beating until light and fluffy. Add eggs, one at a time, beating well after each addition.

Combine flour and soda; add to creamed mixture alternately with buttermilk, beginning and ending with flour mixture. Stir in vanilla.

Pour batter into a greased and floured 10-inch tube pan. Bake at 350° for 1 hour and 20 minutes or until a wooden pick inserted in center comes out clean.

Cool in pan 10 minutes; remove and cool completely. Yield: one 10-inch cake.

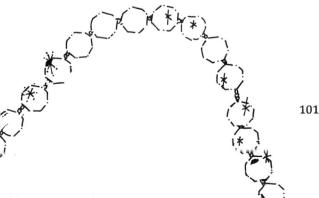

SPECIAL CHOCOLATE CAKE

- 2 (1-ounce) squares unsweetened chocolate
- 3 tablespoons water
- ¾ cup butter or margarine, softened
- 2¼ cups sugar
- 4 eggs, separated
- 1 teaspoon vanilla extract
- 2¼ cups sifted cake flour
- 1 teaspoon cream of tartar
- ½ teaspoon baking soda
- ½ teaspoon salt
- 1 cup milk
  Vanilla Cream Filling
  Chocolate-Cream Cheese Frosting
- ¼ cup chopped almonds, toasted

Combine chocolate and water in a small saucepan; cook over low heat, stirring constantly, until chocolate melts. Cool slightly.

Cream butter; gradually add sugar, beating well. Add egg yolks, one at a time, beating well after each addition. Add chocolate mixture and vanilla; mix well.

Combine flour, cream of tartar, soda, and salt; add to creamed mixture alternately with milk, beginning and ending with flour mixture. Mix well after each addition. Beat egg whites (at room temperature) until stiff peaks form; fold into batter.

Pour batter into 3 greased and floured 9-inch round cakepans; bake at 350° for 25 to 30 minutes or until a wooden pick inserted in center comes out clean. Cool in pans 10 minutes; remove layers from pans, and let cool completely.

Spread Vanilla Cream Filling between layers. Spread Chocolate-Cream Cheese Frosting on top and sides of cake. Sprinkle almonds over top of cake, if desired. Chill cake 3 to 4 hours before serving. Yield: one 3-layer cake.

Vanilla Cream Filling:

- ½ cup sugar
- 3 tablespoons all-purpose flour
- ⅛ teaspoon salt
- 1½ cups milk
- 2 eggs, beaten
- ¼ cup chopped almonds, toasted
- ½ teaspoon vanilla extract

Combine sugar, flour, and salt in a heavy saucepan; gradually stir in milk. Cook over medium heat, stirring constantly, until smooth and thickened. Gradually stir about one-fourth of hot mixture into eggs; add to remaining hot mixture, stirring constantly. Bring to a boil; cook, stirring constantly, 2 to 3 minutes or until thickened. Remove from heat; stir in almonds and vanilla. Cover and chill 1 to 2 hours. Yield: enough for one 3-layer cake.

Chocolate Cream Cheese Frosting:

- 3 (1-ounce) squares unsweetened chocolate
- ¼ cup butter or margarine, softened
- 1 (8-ounce) package cream cheese, softened
- 3 cups sifted powdered sugar, divided
- 1 tablespoon plus 1 teaspoon whipping cream
  Dash of salt
- ½ teaspoon vanilla extract

Melt chocolate in a heavy saucepan over low heat, stirring constantly; cool.

Cream butter and cream cheese; add 1 cup powdered sugar, chocolate, whipping cream, salt, and vanilla, beating well. Add remaining sugar; beat until spreading consistency. Yield: enough for one 3-layer cake.

Chocolate lovers will find a touch of heaven in every bite of our super chocolate cakes. Front to back: Chocolate Caramel Cake and Special Chocolate Cake.

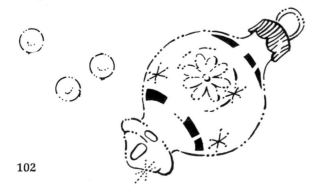

CHOCOLATE CARAMEL CAKE

   3 (1-ounce) squares unsweetened
       chocolate
   ⅔ cup butter or margarine, softened
1½ cups sugar
   ½ cup firmly packed brown sugar
   3 eggs
2⅓ cups sifted cake flour
   2 teaspoons baking soda
   ½ teaspoon salt
1⅓ cups buttermilk
   ⅓ cup water
1¼ teaspoons vanilla extract
       Creamy Caramel Filling
   ½ cup chopped pecans, divided
       Fluffy Marshmallow Frosting
   2 (1-ounce) squares unsweetened
       chocolate (optional)
       Shaved chocolate (optional)

Melt 3 squares chocolate in a heavy saucepan over low heat, stirring constantly; cool slightly.

Cream butter; gradually add sugar and brown sugar, beating until light and fluffy. Add chocolate; mix well. Add eggs, one at a time, beating well after each addition.

Combine flour, soda, and salt; add to creamed mixture alternately with buttermilk, beginning and ending with flour mixture. Mix well after each addition. Stir in water and vanilla.

Pour batter into 3 greased and floured 9-inch round cakepans. Bake at 350° for 25 to 30 minutes or until a wooden pick inserted in center comes out clean. Cool in pans 10 minutes; remove layers from pans, and let cool completely.

Spread half of Caramel Filling on top of one cake layer; sprinkle with ¼ cup pecans. Carefully spread a ½-inch-thick layer of Fluffy Marshmallow Frosting over pecans; place second cake layer on top. Repeat filling, pecan, and frosting layers; top with remaining cake layer. Spread remaining frosting over top and sides of cake.

For an easy—yet spectacular—finish for Chocolate Caramel Cake, drizzle melted chocolate around the edge of the cake. First, melt two squares of chocolate; cool slightly. Carefully spoon the chocolate around the cake, letting the chocolate slide to varying lengths down the sides of the cake.

If desired, melt 2 squares chocolate in a heavy saucepan over low heat, stirring constantly; cool slightly. Drizzle melted chocolate around edges and down sides of cake. Sprinkle shaved chocolate over center of cake, if desired. Yield: one 3-layer cake.

Caramel Filling:

   1 cup firmly packed brown sugar
   3 tablespoons all-purpose flour
   1 cup evaporated milk
   2 egg yolks, slightly beaten
   2 tablespoons butter or margarine

Combine sugar and flour in a saucepan; gradually stir in milk. Cook over medium heat, stirring constantly, until mixture thickens and boils. Boil 1 minute, stirring constantly; remove from heat. Gradually stir about one-fourth of hot mixture into yolks; add to remaining hot mixture, stirring constantly. Return to a boil and boil 1 minute, stirring constantly. Remove from heat; add butter, stirring until butter melts. Let cool. Yield: about 2½ cups.

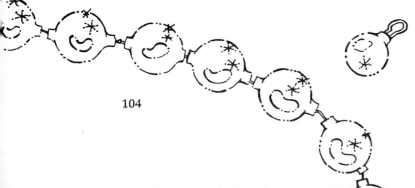

Fluffy Marshmallow Frosting:

- 2 egg whites
- 1½ cups sugar
- 1 tablespoon plus 2 teaspoons light corn syrup
- ⅓ cup water
- 16 large marshmallows, quartered

Combine egg whites (at room temperature), sugar, corn syrup, and water in top of a double boiler; beat 1 minute on high speed of electric mixer. Place over boiling water and beat on high speed of electric mixer 7 minutes. Remove from heat; transfer to a large mixing bowl. Add marshmallows; beat until spreading consistency. Yield: enough for one 3-layer cake.

ORANGE-DATE CAKE

- 1 cup butter or margarine, softened
- 2 cups sugar
- 4 eggs
- 4 cups all-purpose flour, divided
- 1 teaspoon baking soda
- ¼ teaspoon salt
- 1½ cups buttermilk
- 1 (8-ounce) package chopped dates
- 1 cup chopped pecans or walnuts
- 2 tablespoons grated orange rind
- Orange glaze (recipe follows)

Cream butter; gradually add sugar, beating until light and fluffy. Add eggs, one at a time, beating well after each addition.

Combine 3¾ cups flour, soda, and salt; gradually add to creamed mixture alternately with buttermilk, beginning and ending with flour mixture. Mix well after each addition. Dredge dates and pecans in remaining ¼ cup flour; stir into batter.

Pour batter into a greased and floured 10-inch tube pan; sprinkle top with orange rind. Bake at 325° about 1½ hours or until a wooden pick inserted in center comes out clean.

Use a wooden pick to punch holes in top of cake; then, while cake is still hot, pour orange glaze over top. Let cake cool before removing from pan. Yield: one 10-inch cake.

Orange Glaze:

- ½ cup sugar
- 1 tablespoon grated orange rind
- ¼ cup plus 2 tablespoons orange juice
- 1 tablespoon lemon juice

Combine all ingredients in a small saucepan, stirring well. Cook over low heat just until sugar dissolves. Yield: about ⅔ cup.

REGAL FRUITCAKE

- ½ pound candied red cherries, chopped
- ½ pound candied green cherries, chopped
- 1½ cups coarsely chopped pecans
- 1 (7-ounce) can flaked coconut
- 4¼ cups all-purpose flour, divided
- 1¼ cups butter or margarine, softened
- 2 cups sugar
- 6 eggs
- 2 teaspoons baking powder
- ½ teaspoon salt
- ½ cup orange juice

Grease 10-inch tube pan; line with brown paper and grease. Set aside. Combine first 4 ingredients. Dredge with ¼ cup flour; set aside. Cream butter in large bowl; gradually add sugar; beat until light and fluffy. Add eggs, one at a time; beat well after each addition.

Combine remaining 4 cups flour, baking powder, and salt; add to creamed mixture alternately with orange juice, beginning and ending with flour mixture. Mix well after each addition. Stir in fruit mixture.

Spoon batter into prepared pan. Bake at 300° for 2½ hours or until a wooden pick inserted in center comes out clean. Cool in pan 20 minutes before removing; peel paper liner from cake. Cool completely on wire rack. Yield: one 10-inch cake.

Confections

WHITE CHOCOLATE SALTIES

    1 pound white chocolate
    2 tablespoons shortening
    3 cups pretzel sticks
    1 cup salted Spanish peanuts

Combine chocolate and shortening in top of a double boiler; bring water to a boil. Reduce heat to low; cook until chocolate melts. Pour chocolate mixture into a large mixing bowl. Stir in pretzels and peanuts; spread into a buttered 15- × 10- × 1-inch jellyroll pan. Chill 20 minutes or until firm; break into pieces. Store in an airtight container. Yield: 1½ pounds.

OLD-FASHIONED CARAMELS

    2 cups sugar
    1 cup butter or margarine
    1¾ cups light corn syrup
    2 cups whipping cream, divided
    1 teaspoon vanilla extract

Combine first 3 ingredients and 1 cup whipping cream in a heavy saucepan; mix well. Bring to a boil over medium heat; boil gently 1 minute. Stir in remaining whipping cream; bring to a boil over medium heat. Boil gently, stirring occasionally, until mixture reaches soft ball stage (240°). Remove from heat; stir in vanilla.

Pour into a buttered 13- × 9- × 2-inch dish; cover and chill 8 hours or overnight. Remove from refrigerator; let stand 15 minutes. Cut into ¾-inch squares; wrap individually in plastic wrap or decorative cellophane wrappers. Store in refrigerator. Yield: about 9 dozen.

Fill your kitchen with sweet candy-store aromas as you make these delectable confections. Center: Old-Fashioned Caramels. Clockwise from center front: Chocolate Covered Cherries, Butter-Nut Crunchies, White Chocolate Salties, Nutty Candy Squares, and Pecan Brittle.

NUTTY CANDY SQUARES

    2 cups sugar
    1 cup milk
    ¼ teaspoon ground cardamom
    1 tablespoon butter or margarine
    ½ cup slivered almonds, toasted
    ½ cup chopped cashews
    1 cup flaked coconut
    Whole almonds, toasted (optional)

Combine sugar, milk, and cardamom in a Dutch oven; mix well. Cook over medium heat, stirring constantly, until sugar dissolves. Continue cooking over medium heat, stirring occasionally, until mixture reaches soft ball stage (234°). Remove from heat; add butter (do not stir). Cool to lukewarm (110°).

Beat with a wooden spoon 1 minute; stir in slivered almonds, cashews, and coconut. Pour into a buttered 8-inch square pan. Mark warm candy into 1⅓-inch squares; arrange whole almonds in center of squares, if desired. Cool completely and cut. Yield: about 3 dozen.

PECAN BRITTLE

    1 cup sugar
    ½ cup light corn syrup
    ¼ cup water
    ¼ teaspoon salt
    1 cup coarsely chopped pecans
    1 tablespoon butter or margarine
    1 teaspoon baking soda
    ⅓ cup chopped mixed candied fruit

Combine first 4 ingredients in a heavy saucepan; mix well. Cook over medium heat, stirring constantly, until mixture boils and sugar dissolves. Add pecans; return to a boil and cook, stirring frequently, until mixture reaches hard crack stage (300°). Remove from heat; immediately stir in butter and soda.

Quickly spread mixture thinly into a buttered 15- × 10- × 1-inch jellyroll pan. Sprinkle with candied fruit; gently press fruit with back of spoon into candy mixture. Let cool; break into pieces. Yield: About 1 pound.

BUTTER-NUT CRUNCHIES

1 cup sugar
½ cup butter or margarine
¼ cup water
½ teaspoon salt
1½ cups walnuts, finely chopped and divided
1 (12-ounce) package semisweet chocolate morsels

Combine sugar, butter, water, and salt in a heavy saucepan; mix well. Bring to a boil; cook, stirring occasionally, until mixture reaches soft crack stage (285°). Stir in ½ cup walnuts. Pour mixture into a buttered 15- × 10- × 1-inch jellyroll pan, spreading to about ¼-inch thickness. Let cool.

Melt chocolate morsels in a heavy saucepan over low heat, stirring constantly; spread half of chocolate over cooled candy mixture. Sprinkle with ½ cup walnuts; lightly press walnuts into chocolate. Cool until firm. Invert candy; repeat procedure with remaining chocolate and walnuts. Let cool; break into pieces. Store in an airtight container. Yield: About 1 pound.

CHOCOLATE COVERED CHERRIES

¼ cup butter or margarine, softened
2½ cups sifted powdered sugar
1 tablespoon milk
½ teaspoon vanilla extract
⅛ teaspoon almond extract
About 42 maraschino cherries with stems
1 (6-ounce) package semisweet chocolate morsels
½ (8-ounce) milk chocolate bar, broken into pieces
1 tablespoon shortening

Cream butter; gradually add sugar, beating well. Blend in milk and flavorings.

Drain cherries; dry on absorbent paper towels. Shape a small amount of sugar mixture around each cherry. Place on waxed paper-lined cookie sheet; chill 2 hours or until firm.

Melt remaining ingredients in top of a double boiler. Dip each cherry by the stem into chocolate. Place on a waxed paper-lined cookie sheet; chill until firm. Store in a cool place. Yield: About 3½ dozen.

PEANUT RIPPLE DIVINITY

3 cups sugar
½ cup water
½ cup light corn syrup
2 egg whites
1 teaspoon vanilla extract
½ cup peanut butter chips
½ cup roasted peanuts, chopped

Combine sugar, water, and syrup in a 3-quart saucepan; cook over low heat, stirring constantly, until sugar dissolves. Cook over high heat, without stirring, until mixture reaches hard ball stage (260°).

Beat egg whites (at room temperature) in a large mixing bowl until stiff peaks form. Pour hot sugar mixture in a very thin stream over egg whites while beating at high speed of an electric mixer. Add vanilla, and continue beating until mixture holds its shape (5 to 7 minutes). Stir in the remaining ingredients.

Drop by teaspoonfuls onto waxed paper; let stand until firm. Yield: About 3½ dozen.

PEANUT BUTTER DELIGHTS

- 2 cups sugar
- 3 tablespoons cocoa
- ½ cup milk
- ½ cup butter or margarine
- 1 tablespoon vanilla extract
- 1 cup creamy peanut butter
- 3 cups quick-cooking oats, uncooked

Combine first 5 ingredients in a heavy saucepan; mix well. Bring to a boil; boil 1 minute, stirring occasionally. Remove from heat; stir in peanut butter. Add oats; mix well. Quickly drop by heaping teaspoonfuls onto waxed paper; cool. Yield: About 5½ dozen.

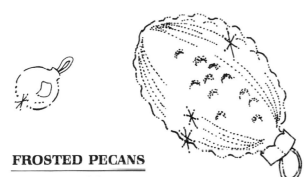

FROSTED PECANS

- 1 egg white
- 2 tablespoons cold water
- ⅛ teaspoon salt
- ½ teaspoon ground cinnamon
- ¼ teaspoon ground cloves
- ¼ teaspoon ground allspice
- ½ cup sugar
- 2 cups pecan halves

Combine egg white (at room temperature), water, salt, and spices; beat until foamy. Gradually add sugar, 1 tablespoon at a time, beating until stiff peaks form. Dip pecan halves, one at a time, into egg white mixture. Place pecan halves an inch apart on greased baking sheets. Bake at 275° for 40 to 45 minutes. Store in an airtight container. Yield: 2½ cups.

COCONUT CONES

- 1 cup sugar
- ½ cup molasses
- ¼ cup sweetened condensed milk
- ¼ cup light corn syrup
- ¼ cup water
- ¼ teaspoon salt
- 2 tablespoons shortening
- 1 pound flaked coconut

Combine first 6 ingredients in a heavy saucepan; mix well. Cook over medium heat, stirring frequently, until mixture reaches soft ball stage (234°). Add shortening; stir until melted. Stir in coconut. Pour into a buttered 15- × 10- × 1-inch jellyroll pan; cool to touch. Shape into 1¼-inch tall cones; chill 3 to 4 hours. Store in an airtight container in refrigerator. Yield: 5½ dozen.

OVERNIGHT MERINGUES

- 2 egg whites
- ½ cup sugar
- 1 teaspoon almond extract
- ¼ teaspoon vanilla extract
- 1 cup chopped pecans
- 1 cup semisweet chocolate morsels

Beat egg whites (at room temperature) until foamy. Gradually add sugar, 1 tablespoon at a time, beating until stiff peaks form. Add flavorings; mix well. Fold in pecans and chocolate morsels.

Drop by heaping teaspoonfuls onto aluminum foil-lined cookie sheets. Place in a 350° oven; immediately turn oven off. Let stand 8 to 10 hours or overnight. (Do not open oven.) Store in an airtight container. Yield: 5 dozen.

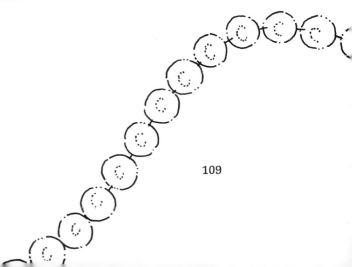

Cookies

MADELEINES

- 2 eggs
- ⅛ teaspoon salt
- ⅓ cup sugar
- ½ cup all-purpose flour
- 1 teaspoon grated lemon rind
- ½ cup butter, melted and cooled
  Powdered sugar

Beat eggs and salt until foamy. Gradually add sugar; beat 15 minutes at high speed of an electric mixer or until thick and lemon-colored. Fold in flour, 2 tablespoons at a time, and lemon rind. Fold in butter, 1 tablespoon at a time. Spoon 1 tablespoon batter into greased and floured madeleine molds. Bake at 400° for 8 to 10 minutes or until

lightly browned. Remove from molds and cool on a wire rack, flat side down. Sprinkle with powdered sugar. Yield: 1 dozen.

PAINTED CHRISTMAS COOKIES

- ½ cup butter or margarine, softened
- ½ cup shortening
- 1 cup sifted powdered sugar
- 1 egg
- 1 teaspoon vanilla extract
- 2½ cups all-purpose flour
- 1 teaspoon salt
  Egg Yolk Paint

Cream butter and shortening; gradually add sugar, beating well. Add egg and vanilla; beat well.

Combine flour and salt; stir into creamed mixture. Divide dough in half; wrap in waxed paper and chill at least 1 hour.

Roll half of dough to ⅛-inch thickness on a lightly floured large cookie sheet; keep remaining dough chilled. Cut dough into desired shapes; remove excess dough. Using a small paintbrush, paint assorted designs on cookies with Egg Yolk Paint.

Bake at 375° for 9 to 10 minutes or until cookies are lightly browned. Remove from cookie sheet and let cool completely on a wire rack. Repeat with remaining dough. Yield: 2½ dozen (3-inch) cookies.

Egg Yolk Paint:

- 1 egg yolk
- ¼ teaspoon water
  Assorted colors of paste food coloring

Combine egg yolk and water; mix well. Divide mixture into several custard cups; tint as desired with paste food coloring. Keep paint covered until ready to use. If paint thickens, add a few drops of water and mix well. Yield: 1½ tablespoons.

When making Painted Christmas Cookies, roll out the cookies on a lightly floured cookie sheet and cut out with round cookie cutters. Lightly press a decorative cutter into each round, leaving only a slight imprint of the design. These imprints become the outline for your paintings.

This recipe for Painted Christmas Cookies can also be used for cut-out cookies that are decorated with Royal Icing. Use your favorite cookie cutters and decorate with icing and assorted candies and sprinkles.

ROYAL ICING

- 3 large egg whites
- ½ teaspoon cream of tartar
- 1 (16-ounce) package powdered sugar, sifted
- Red and green paste food coloring

Combine egg whites (at room temperature) and cream of tartar in a large mixing bowl. Beat at medium speed with an electric mixer until frothy. Gradually add powdered sugar, mixing well. Beat 5 to 7 minutes. Color portions of icing with paste food coloring, if desired. Prepare decorating bags, and decorate as desired. (Icing dries very quickly; keep covered at all times with plastic wrap.) Yield: about 2 cups.

LEMON BONBONS

- 1 cup butter, softened
- ⅓ cup sifted powdered sugar
- 1¼ cups all-purpose flour
- ¾ cup cornstarch
- ½ cup finely chopped pecans
- 1½ cups sifted powdered sugar
- 1½ teaspoons butter or margarine, softened
- 1½ tablespoons lemon juice

Cream 1 cup butter; gradually add ⅓ cup powdered sugar, beating well. Add flour and cornstarch; mix well. Cover and chill 1 hour. Shape dough into 1-inch balls; lightly coat each with pecans. Flatten each cookie with the bottom of a glass which has been lightly dipped in flour. Place on ungreased cookie sheets; bake at 350° for 12 to 14 minutes. Cool on wire racks.

Combine 1½ cups powdered sugar, 1½ teaspoons butter, and lemon juice; mix until smooth. Spread on cookies. Yield: 2½ dozen.

You'll need lots of these irresistible cookies for those hungry holiday guests. Front to back: Lemon Bonbons, Painted Christmas Cookies, and Chocolate Drops.

CHOCOLATE DROPS

  2 (1-ounce) squares unsweetened
     chocolate
  ½ cup shortening
1⅔ cups firmly packed brown sugar
  2 eggs
  1 teaspoon vanilla extract
  2 cups all-purpose flour
  2 teaspoons baking powder
  1 teaspoon ground cinnamon
  ¾ teaspoon salt
  ⅓ cup milk
  ⅔ cup chopped pecans
     Powdered sugar

Melt chocolate in a heavy saucepan over low heat; cool.

Cream shortening and sugar, beating well. Add eggs, one at a time, beating well after each addition. Add chocolate and vanilla; mix well. Combine flour, baking powder, cinnamon, and salt; add to creamed mixture alternately with milk, beginning and ending with flour mixture. Stir in pecans. Cover and chill at least 2 hours.

Coat hands lightly with powdered sugar. Shape dough into 1-inch balls and roll in powdered sugar. Place 2 inches apart on greased cookie sheets; chill 30 minutes. Bake at 350° for 20 minutes. Remove from cookie sheets while warm; cool on wire racks. Yield: 5 dozen.

DEVILS FOOD COOKIES

  ½ cup shortening
  1 cup sugar
  2 eggs
1¾ cups all-purpose flour
  ½ cup cocoa
  1 teaspoon baking soda
  ½ teaspoon salt
  1 teaspoon vanilla extract
  1 teaspoon butter flavoring
     About 20 large marshmallows, cut
      in half
     Chocolate Frosting (recipe follows)

Cream shortening and sugar, beating well. Add eggs, one at a time, beating well after each addition.

Combine next 4 ingredients, mixing well; add to creamed mixture, beating well. Stir in flavorings. (Dough will be stiff.) Chill dough at least 30 minutes.

Shape dough into 1-inch balls; place on greased cookie sheets. Bake at 350° for 8 minutes. Place a marshmallow half on top of each cookie; bake an additional 2 minutes. Cool on wire racks, and frost with Chocolate Frosting. Yield: about 3½ dozen.

Chocolate Frosting:

  ½ cup semisweet chocolate morsels
  ¼ cup milk
  2 tablespoons butter or margarine
  2 cups sifted powdered sugar

Combine first 3 ingredients in a saucepan; cook, stirring constantly, over low heat, until chocolate melts. Add powdered sugar, beating until smooth. Add additional milk, if needed, for proper spreading consistency. Yield: 1 cup.

CARAMEL SAND TARTS

  ½ cup butter, softened
  1 cup firmly packed brown sugar
  1 egg
  1 teaspoon vanilla extract
1½ cups all-purpose flour
  2 teaspoons baking powder
  ¼ teaspoon salt
  1 egg white
2½ dozen pecan halves
  1 tablespoon sugar
  ¼ teaspoon ground cinnamon

Cream butter; gradually add brown sugar, beating until light and fluffy. Add egg and vanilla; mix well. Combine flour, baking powder, and salt; stir into creamed mixture. Cover and chill 1 to 2 hours.

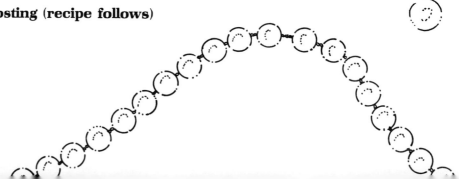

Roll dough to ⅛-inch thickness on a lightly floured surface; cut into rounds with a 2½-inch cookie cutter. Place on greased cookie sheets. Brush each cookie cutout with egg white. Combine sugar and cinnamon; sprinkle lightly over cookies. Lightly press a pecan half in center of each. Bake at 350° for 8 to 10 minutes or until lightly browned. Yield: 2½ dozen.

ORANGE COOKIE MIX

- 1 cup sugar
- 1 cup firmly packed brown sugar
- 1 cup shortening
- 2 cups all-purpose flour
- 1 teaspoon baking powder
- 1 teaspoon baking soda
- 1 teaspoon ground cinnamon
- ¼ teaspoon salt
- 2 cups quick-cooking oats
- 2 cups corn flakes

Combine sugar in a large bowl; cut in shortening with a pastry blender until mixture resembles coarse meal. Combine remaining ingredients, and mix well. Stir into sugar mixture. Cover and store in refrigerator. Yield: 8 cups.

Orange-Nut Cookies:

- 2 cups Orange Cookie Mix
- 1 egg, slightly beaten
- 2 to 3 teaspoons grated orange rind
- 1 tablespoon plus 1 teaspoon orange juice
- ½ cup chopped walnuts

Combine all ingredients, mixing well. Shape dough into 1-inch balls; place about 2 inches apart on ungreased cookie sheets. Bake at 375° for 10 to 12 minutes. Yield: about 2½ dozen.

CHRISTMAS PIES

- ½ cup shortening
- 1 cup sugar
- 1 egg
- 1 egg yolk
- 2 cups all-purpose flour
- ⅔ cup cocoa
- ½ teaspoon salt
- 1 teaspoon baking soda
- ½ cup hot water
- ⅔ cup buttermilk
- Filling (recipe follows)

Cream shortening and sugar, beating well. Add egg and egg yolk, beating well.

Combine flour, cocoa, and salt; stir well. Dissolve soda in hot water; cool slightly. Add flour mixture to creamed mixture, alternately with soda mixture and buttermilk, beginning and ending with dry ingredients.

Drop batter by heaping tablespoons, 2 inches apart, onto ungreased cookie sheets. Bake at 350° for 10 to 12 minutes. Remove immediately from cookie sheets; cool on wire racks.

Spread filling on flat side of half the cookies; top with remaining cookies. Yield: 1 dozen.

Filling:

- ½ cup shortening
- ¼ cup butter or margarine, softened
- 2 cups sifted powdered sugar
- 1 egg white
- 1 teaspoon vanilla extract

Cream shortening and butter; gradually add sugar, beating until light and fluffy. Add egg white and vanilla, beating until smooth and creamy. Yield: 1½ cups.

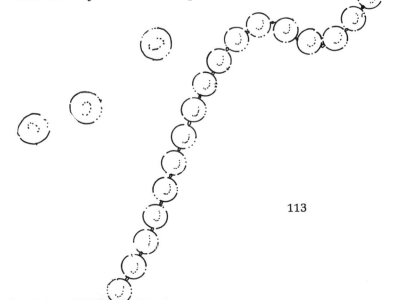

Gift Ideas

HOMEMADE COFFEE LIQUEUR

    2 cups water
    4 cups dark corn syrup
    1 cup light corn syrup
    ¼ cup plus 2 tablespoons instant
        coffee granules
    1 (25.4-ounce) bottle vodka
    1 (25.4-ounce) bottle light rum
    1 (2-ounce) bottle vanilla extract

Combine first 4 ingredients in a Dutch oven;
bring to a boil. Reduce heat, and simmer 1
hour, stirring often; cool completely. Stir in
vodka, rum, and vanilla. Store in airtight
containers. Yield: 3 quarts.

Note: Use in beverages as you would use
Kahlúa, or serve over ice cream or as an
ingredient in desserts.

PEANUT-BUTTERSCOTCH SAUCE

    1½ cups firmly packed brown sugar
    ⅔ cup light corn syrup
    ¼ cup butter or margarine
    ⅛ teaspoon salt
    1 (5.33-ounce) can evaporated milk
    ¼ cup creamy peanut butter
    ½ cup coarsely chopped peanuts

Combine sugar, corn syrup, and butter in a
heavy saucepan; stir well. Cook over medium heat, stirring constantly, until mixture
reaches soft ball stage (234°). Remove from
heat; stir in remaining ingredients. Serve
over vanilla ice cream. Store in airtight container in refrigerator. Sauce may be re-
heated. Yield: 2¼ cups.

JEZEBEL SAUCE

    1 (18-ounce) jar pineapple preserves
    1 (18-ounce) jar apple jelly
    3 tablespoons dry mustard
    ½ cup plus 2 tablespoons prepared
        horseradish
    1 tablespoon coarsely ground
        pepper

Combine all ingredients; stir well. Pour
sauce into an airtight container; store in
refrigerator. Serve sauce over cream cheese
with crackers as an appetizer or with pork
or beef. Yield: 3½ cups.

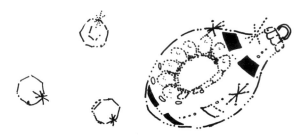

HOLIDAY PINEAPPLE SAUCE

    2 (15¼-ounce) cans crushed
        pineapple, undrained
    ⅔ cup light corn syrup
    3 tablespoons crème de menthe

Combine pineapple and corn syrup in a
heavy saucepan; cook over medium heat,
stirring frequently, until liquid evaporates.
Let cool. Stir in crème de menthe; serve over
vanilla ice cream. Store in airtight container
in refrigerator. Yield: About 2 cups.

*For holiday gift giving, try our
straight-from-the-kitchen ideas. Back, left to
right: Crunchy Granola, Peppy Pepper Jelly, Hot
Mustard, and Jezebel Sauce. Center:
Peanut-Butterscotch Sauce, Holiday Pineapple
Sauce, and Homemade Coffee Liqueur. Front:
Popcorn Cake Delight.*

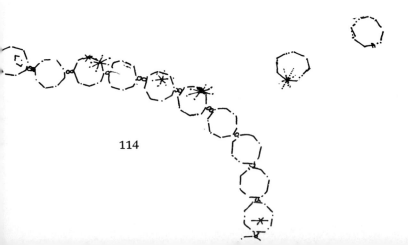

CRUNCHY GRANOLA

4 cups regular oats, uncooked
1 cup wheat germ
1 cup flaked coconut
1 cup sunflower kernels
1 cup chopped almonds
½ cup sesame seeds
1 teaspoon salt
½ cup honey
½ cup vegetable oil
1 tablespoon vanilla extract
1 cup chopped dates
½ cup raisins
½ cup mixed dried fruit, chopped

Combine first 7 ingredients in a large bowl; mix well, and set aside. Combine honey, oil, and vanilla in a small saucepan; place over medium heat, and cook, stirring constantly until mixture is thoroughly heated. Pour over oats mixture; mix well.

Spread oats mixture evenly into a lightly greased 15- × 10- × 1-inch jellyroll pan; bake at 350° for 20 to 25 minutes or until golden, stirring every 5 minutes. Remove from oven; stir in dates, raisins, and dried fruit. Cool; store in an airtight container. Serve with milk as cereal or as a snack. Yield: 10 cups.

PEPPY PEPPER JELLY

6 large red peppers, seeded and coarsely chopped
1 (4-ounce) can chopped jalapeño peppers, drained
1½ cups cider vinegar
1½ cups apple juice
¾ teaspoon salt
2 (1¾-ounce) packages dry fruit pectin
5 cups sugar

Combine half each of the red peppers, jalapeño peppers and vinegar in container of electric blender; process until puréed. Repeat with remaining peppers and vinegar;

stir in apple juice. Cover and let stand 8 hours or overnight.

Strain puréed mixture through a jelly bag or 4 layers of cheesecloth, reserving 4 cups juice. Discard pulp.

Combine prepared juice, salt, and pectin in a large Dutch oven; bring to a rolling boil, stirring frequently. Add sugar all at once; stir well and return to a rolling boil. Continue boiling 1 minute, stirring frequently. Remove from heat, and skim off foam with a metal spoon.

Quickly pour the jelly into sterilized jars, leaving ¼-inch headspace; cover at once with metal lids, and screw bands tight. Process in boiling-water bath for 5 minutes. Yield: 6 half pints.

FRUITCAKE DELIGHT

1½ cups all-purpose flour
1 teaspoon baking powder
½ teaspoon salt
1½ cups sugar
2 (8-ounce) packages pitted dates, chopped
2 (8-ounce) cans crushed pineapple, drained
2 (16-ounce) jars maraschino cherries, drained and chopped
1 (15-ounce) package raisins
5 cups chopped pecans
6 eggs
⅓ cup dark rum or pineapple juice
¼ cup light corn syrup

Grease bottom of two 9- × - 5- × 3-inch loafpans; line bottoms with waxed paper. Grease and flour waxed paper and sides of pans; set aside.

Combine flour, baking powder, salt, and sugar; mix well. Stir in fruit and pecans. Combine eggs and rum; beat well. Stir into flour mixture.

Spoon batter into prepared pans, pressing batter with back of spoon to pack firmly. Bake at 300° for 1 hour and 45 minutes or until a wooden pick inserted in center comes out clean. Cool in pans 10 minutes; remove from pans, and peel off paper liner. Brush tops and sides of warm loaves with corn syrup; cool. Yield: two loaves.

POPCORN CAKE DELIGHT

   8 cups freshly popped popcorn,
      unsalted
   ¾ cup sugar
   ¾ cup firmly packed brown sugar
   ½ cup light corn syrup
   ½ cup water
   1 teaspoon vinegar
   ¼ teaspoon salt
   ¾ cup butter or margarine
   1 cup candy-coated chocolate pieces
   1 cup Spanish peanuts
   1 cup miniature marshmallows

Place popcorn in a large bowl; set aside.

Combine next 6 ingredients in a large saucepan. Cook over medium heat, stirring frequently, until mixture reaches hard ball stage (260°). Remove from heat; add butter, stirring until butter melts.

Pour syrup in a thin stream over popcorn, stirring until popcorn is evenly coated. Stir in remaining ingredients, mixing well. Press mixture into a well-greased 6-cup ring mold; cool. Unmold on serving plate. Yield: one popcorn ring.

HOT MUSTARD

   2 (2-ounce) cans dry mustard
   1 cup vinegar
   1 cup sugar
   1 teaspoon salt
   2 eggs, beaten

Combine mustard and vinegar in top of a double boiler; stir well. Cover and let stand 8 hours or overnight. Add remaining ingredients; mix well. Place over boiling water and cook 3 to 5 minutes, stirring constantly until thickened. Store in airtight containers in refrigerator. Yield: 2 cups.

CANDIED ORANGE PEEL

   2 large naval oranges
   ½ cup sugar
   ¼ cup water
   Sugar

Remove peel from oranges and cut into ¼-inch-wide strips. Place orange peel in a large saucepan, and cover with water; bring to a boil. Drain. Repeat boiling procedure 3 times, and set peel aside.

Combine ½ cup sugar and ¼ cup water in a heavy saucepan; bring to a boil and cook, stirring often, until mixture reaches soft ball stage (235°). Add peel; simmer 10 to 15 minutes, stirring often, or until most of liquid evaporates. Drain, if necessary. Cool to touch.

Roll peel, a few pieces at a time, in sugar. Arrange in a single layer on wire racks; let dry 4 to 5 hours. Store in an airtight container. Yield: About ½ pound.

Party Fare

HAM ROLLS

- 1 (3-ounce) package cream cheese, softened
- 2 tablespoons finely chopped green pepper
- 2 tablespoons chopped pimiento, well drained
- 1 tablespoon mayonnaise
- 1½ teaspoons Creole mustard
- 6 (6- × 4- × ⅛-inch) boiled ham slices

Combine all ingredients except ham. Spread cream cheese mixture evenly on one side of each ham slice; roll up and secure with a wooden pick. Cover and chill.

Carefully slice each roll into ½-inch pieces; serve with toothpicks. Yield: 4 dozen.

MINIATURE SAUSAGE QUICHE

- ½ pound mild bulk pork sausage, cooked and drained
- 2 eggs, beaten
- ½ cup milk
- 1½ tablespoons butter, melted
- 1 cup (4 ounces) shredded Cheddar cheese
  - Pastry shells (recipe follows)
  - Paprika
  - Parsley sprigs (optional)

Combine first 5 ingredients; stir well, and pour into prepared pastry shells. Sprinkle with paprika. Bake at 350° for 20 to 25 minutes or until set. Garnish with parsley just before serving, if desired. Yield: 3 dozen.

Pastry Shells:

- 1¾ cups plus 2 tablespoons all-purpose flour
- 1½ teaspoons salt
- 4½ tablespoons butter, melted
- 1 egg yolk
- 5 to 6 tablespoons cold water

Build an eye-catching hors d'oeuvre tray with Ham Rolls and Miniature Sausage Quiche.

Combine flour and salt; add butter, mixing well. Add egg yolk and water; stir with a fork until all dry ingredients are moistened. Shape dough into 36 (1-inch) balls. Place dough balls in lightly greased 1¾-inch muffin pans or assorted canapé tins, shaping each into a shell. Prick bottom and sides of pastry shell with a fork; bake at 400° for 5 minutes. Let cool on a rack. Yield: 3 dozen.

CHICKEN LIVER PATÉ

- 1 pound chicken livers
- 6 cups water
- 3 stalks celery, halved
- ½ teaspoon salt
- 6 peppercorns
- 1 cup butter, cut into pieces
- ⅓ cup chopped onion
- 2 tablespoons brandy
- 1 clove garlic
- ½ teaspoon salt
- 2½ teaspoons dry mustard
- ½ teaspoon ground nutmeg
- ⅛ teaspoon ground cloves
  - Dash of ground red pepper
- ¼ cup currants

Combine chicken livers, water, celery, ½ teaspoon salt, and peppercorns in a medium saucepan; bring to a boil. Reduce heat, cover, and simmer 5 minutes or until tender. Drain livers well; discard celery and peppercorns.

Place livers in container of food processor or electric blender. Add remaining ingredients except currants; process until smooth. Stir in currants. Spoon mixture into an oiled 3-cup mold; cover and chill several hours or overnight. Invert onto platter, and serve with assorted crackers. Yield: 3 cups.

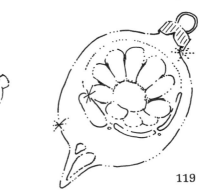

ARTICHOKE SQUARES

2 (6-ounce) jars marinated
  artichokes
1 medium onion, chopped
4 eggs, beaten
¼ cup fine, dry breadcrumbs
½ teaspoon dried whole oregano
¼ teaspoon salt
⅛ teaspoon pepper
  Dash of hot sauce
1 clove garlic, minced
2 cups (8 ounces) shredded Cheddar
  cheese

Drain artichokes, reserving liquid from 1 jar. Chop artichokes; set aside.

Cook onion in reserved liquid in skillet until tender. Combine eggs, breadcrumbs, oregano, salt, pepper, and hot sauce in a large mixing bowl; mix well. Add onion, artichokes, garlic, and cheese; stir well. Pour into a greased 13- × 9- × 2-inch baking pan; bake at 325° for 30 minutes or until set. Cut into squares to serve. Yield: About 4 dozen appetizer servings.

FRIED CAULIFLOWER WITH MUSTARD DIP

2 medium heads cauliflower
2 eggs, beaten
1⅓ cups milk
1⅓ cups all-purpose flour
½ teaspoon salt
¼ teaspoon pepper
1½ to 2 cups cracker meal
  Vegetable oil
  Mustard Dip

Wash cauliflower, and break into flowerets. Combine eggs, milk, flour, salt, and pepper; stir until smooth. Dip flowerets in batter; dredge in cracker meal. Deep fry in hot oil (375°) until golden brown. Serve immediately with Mustard Dip. Yield: About 4 dozen appetizer servings.

Mustard Dip:

1 cup mayonnaise
2 tablespoons grated onion
1 tablespoon Dijon mustard
1 tablespoon white wine vinegar
½ teaspoon curry powder

Combine all ingredients; mix well. Chill 2 to 3 hours. Yield: 1¼ cups.

ITALIAN-STYLE CHEESE BALL

2 (8-ounce) packages cream cheese,
  softened
1 (2.5-ounce) package pressed
  cooked ham, chopped
¼ cup commercial Italian salad
  dressing
  Chopped pecans

Combine all ingredients except pecans; mix well. Shape into a ball; roll in pecans. Serve with assorted crackers. Yield: 1 cheese ball.

GLORIOUS AMARETTO CHEESE DIP

½ (8-ounce) package cream cheese,
  softened
1 cup (4 ounces) shredded sharp
  Cheddar cheese
2 to 3 tablespoons amaretto
1 tablespoon brandy
½ cup finely chopped almonds,
  toasted
  Additional finely chopped almonds,
  toasted (optional)

Combine all ingredients except almonds in a mixing bowl; beat on medium speed of electric mixer until smooth. Stir in ½ cup almonds. Spoon into serving dish; garnish with additional almonds, if desired. Serve with assorted fresh fruit or crackers. Yield: About 1¼ cups.

Assorted fruits of the season make perfect party accompaniments for Glorious Amaretto Cheese Dip.

Better have plenty of Hot Pepper Jelly Turnovers on hand; these cheese pastry treats disappear in a hurry.

HOT PEPPER JELLY TURNOVERS

- 1 (5-ounce) jar sharp process cheese spread
- ½ cup butter or margarine
- 1 cup all-purpose flour
- 1 tablespoon cold water
- 2 tablespoons hot red or green pepper jelly, divided

Cut cheese spread and butter into flour with pastry blender until mixture resembles coarse meal. Sprinkle cold water evenly over surface; stir with a fork until all dry ingredients are moistened. Shape dough into a ball; chill at least 4 hours.

Divide dough in half; keep one portion refrigerated. Roll out half of dough on a heavily floured surface to ¼-inch thickness. Cut into rounds with a 3-inch cookie cutter; place ¼ teaspoon jelly in center of each round. Moisten edges with water. Fold each round in half and press edges with a fork to seal (edges must be well sealed). Place on lightly greased cookie sheets. Repeat process with remaining dough. Bake at 375° for 10 to 12 minutes. Cool turnovers on a wire rack. Yield: About 2 dozen.

122

OVERNIGHT SHRIMP DIP

- 9 cups water
- 3 pounds medium shrimp
- 1 (8-ounce) package cream cheese, softened
- 2 tablespoons fresh lemon juice
- 3 tablespoons salad dressing or mayonnaise
- 1 teaspoon Worcestershire sauce
- 4 drops hot sauce
- ½ teaspoon salt
- ¼ teaspoon pepper
- ⅓ to ½ cup minced green onion

Bring water to a boil; add shrimp and return to a boil. Reduce heat, and simmer 3 to 5 minutes. Drain well; rinse with cold water. Chill. Peel and devein shrimp; chop. Set aside.

Combine cream cheese, lemon juice, salad dressing, Worcestershire sauce, hot sauce, salt, and pepper; mix well. Stir in shrimp and onion; cover and chill 8 hours or overnight. Serve with assorted crackers. Yield: About 4 cups.

ROMANO-SHRIMP STUFFED MUSHROOMS

- About 20 large fresh mushrooms
- 1 (4¼-ounce) can shrimp, rinsed, drained, and chopped
- 1 (4-ounce) carton soft cream cheese with chives
- ½ teaspoon Worcestershire sauce
  Dash of garlic powder
- 2 or 3 drops hot sauce
  About ¼ cup grated Romano cheese

Clean mushrooms with damp paper towels. Remove stems and reserve for later use. Set caps aside. Combine remaining ingredients except Romano cheese; mix well. Spoon into mushroom caps; sprinkle with Romano cheese. Place mushrooms in a lightly greased 11- × 7- × 2-inch baking pan; cover and chill 2 to 3 hours. Uncover; bake at 400° for 15 minutes. Yield: about 20 appetizers.

Christmas Journal

Somewhere between memory and anticipation, there exists the reality of Christmas. Gifts, foods, the tree, decorations, stockings, parties, family gatherings, the visit to Santa, a Christmas story before the fire. Christmas challenges our creativity, urging us to make the best of the season.

Planning is part of the challenge: choosing the best gift, making the house shine with new arrangements, serving scrumptious foods to dear friends, surprising someone with a gift that you made

yourself. In this chapter, you will find a holiday calendar to help you keep your schedule straight. There is a party planner to remind you of the things to consider as you organize small or large gatherings. There are card lists, gift lists, size charts, and mailing tips.

After Christmas, be sure to go through the "Christmas Journal" again and record the happy times and things you want to remember in years to come.

Mailing

CARDS

Keep in mind the following U.S. Postal regulations. Envelopes must be rectangular in shape. Envelopes smaller than 3½″ × 5″ cannot be mailed. Envelopes larger than 6⅛″ × 11½″, even if they weigh less than 1 ounce, require extra postage.

PACKAGES

Before you wrap a package, consider the contents, the sturdiness of the box, the cushioning, and closure with tape.

Choose a sturdy box. Include adequate cushioning. Place your return address and address of the recipient inside the box. Wrap the package in brown paper. Use a filament tape. Masking tape, cellophane tape and surgical tape are just not strong enough. Address clearly.

Packages may be sent through the U.S. Postal Service by parcel post in weights up to 70 pounds and measurements of 108″ of combined length and girth.

United Parcel Service (UPS) accepts packages up to 50 pounds for delivery in state, 70 pounds in interstate shipment, and up to 108″ in combined length and girth. There is a pick-up fee for door-to-door service.

CATEGORY	EXAMPLES	CONTAINER	CUSHIONING	CLOSURE
Soft Goods		Self-supporting box or tear-resistant bag		Reinforced tape or sealed bag
Liquids		Leak proof interior and secondary containers	Absorbent	Sealed with filament tape
Powders		Must be sift-proof		Sealed with filament tape
Perishables		Impermeable to content odor	Absorbent	Sealed with filament tape
Fragile Items		Fiberboard (minimum 175 lb test)	To distribute shocks and separate from container surfaces with foamed plastic or padding	Sealed and reinforced with filament tape
Awkward Loads		Fiberboard tubes and boxes with length not over 10 times girth	Pre-formed fiberboard or foamed plastic shapes	Tube ends equal to side wall strength

CONTAINER	CUSHIONING	CLOSURE		ADDRESSING
Fiberboard Manufacturer's Certificate 125 lb test to 20 lbs 175 lb test to 40 lbs 275 lb test to 70 lbs Paperboard up to 10 lbs	Wrap each item individually with enough padding to prevent damage from shock Separate wrapped items from outer package surfaces with padding or foamed plastic	CLOSURE	Pressure Sensitive Filament Tape is preferable to prevent accidental opening Reinforced Kraft Paper Tape Kraft Paper Tape	Address Labels should be readable from 30″ away and should not be easily smeared or washed off Should contain ZIP Code Return Address should also be included inside of carton

Adapted from a U.S. Postal Service poster.

Gifts & Wishes

125

Size Charts

_____

_____

_____

_____

_____

_____

_____

_____

_____

_____

_____

_____

_____

_____

_____

_____

_____

_____

_____

_____

_____

_____

_____

Name		Name	
height	weight	height	weight
coat	slacks	coat	slacks
dress	pajamas	dress	pajamas
suit	bathrobe	suit	bathrobe
sweater	shoes	sweater	shoes
shirt	hat	shirt	hat
blouse	gloves	blouse	gloves
skirt	ring	skirt	ring

Name		Name	
height	weight	height	weight
coat	slacks	coat	slacks
dress	pajamas	dress	pajamas
suit	bathrobe	suit	bathrobe
sweater	shoes	sweater	shoes
shirt	hat	shirt	hat
blouse	gloves	blouse	gloves
skirt	ring	skirt	ring

Name		Name	
height	weight	height	weight
coat	slacks	coat	slacks
dress	pajamas	dress	pajamas
suit	bathrobe	suit	bathrobe
sweater	shoes	sweater	shoes
shirt	hat	shirt	hat
blouse	gloves	blouse	gloves
skirt	ring	skirt	ring

Name		Name	
height	weight	height	weight
coat	slacks	coat	slacks
dress	pajamas	dress	pajamas
suit	bathrobe	suit	bathrobe
sweater	shoes	sweater	shoes
shirt	hat	shirt	hat
blouse	gloves	blouse	gloves
skirt	ring	skirt	ring

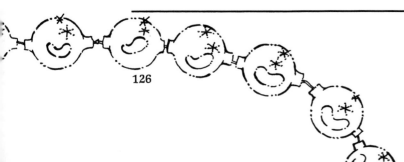

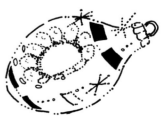

Christmas Card List

CHRISTMAS CARD LIST (CONTINUED)

_____   _____
_____   _____
_____   _____
_____   _____
_____   _____
_____   _____
_____   _____
_____   _____
_____   _____
_____   _____
_____   _____
_____   _____
_____   _____
_____   _____
_____   _____
_____   _____
_____   _____
_____   _____
_____   _____

Holiday Calendar

Christmas ornaments in America began with the Pennsylvania Dutch, who brought with them to America the German tradition of the tree. Prince Albert, husband of Victoria, brought the tradition to England. An engraving of Albert's tabletop tree—laden with baskets and trays of sweets, gilt gingerbread, elaborately decorated cakes and fruits—appeared in the *Illustrated London News* in 1848, and, with a few changes, in *Godey's Lady's Book* in 1850; on both sides of the Atlantic, people rushed to join the tradition. No longer was the tree—with all its ornaments—just a decoration of the Pennsylvania Dutch; it was an accepted custom.

Thursday, November 1

Friday, November 2

Saturday, November 3

Sunday, November 4

Monday, November 5

Tuesday, November 6

Wednesday, November 7

Thursday, November 8

Friday, November 9

Saturday, November 10

Sunday, November 11

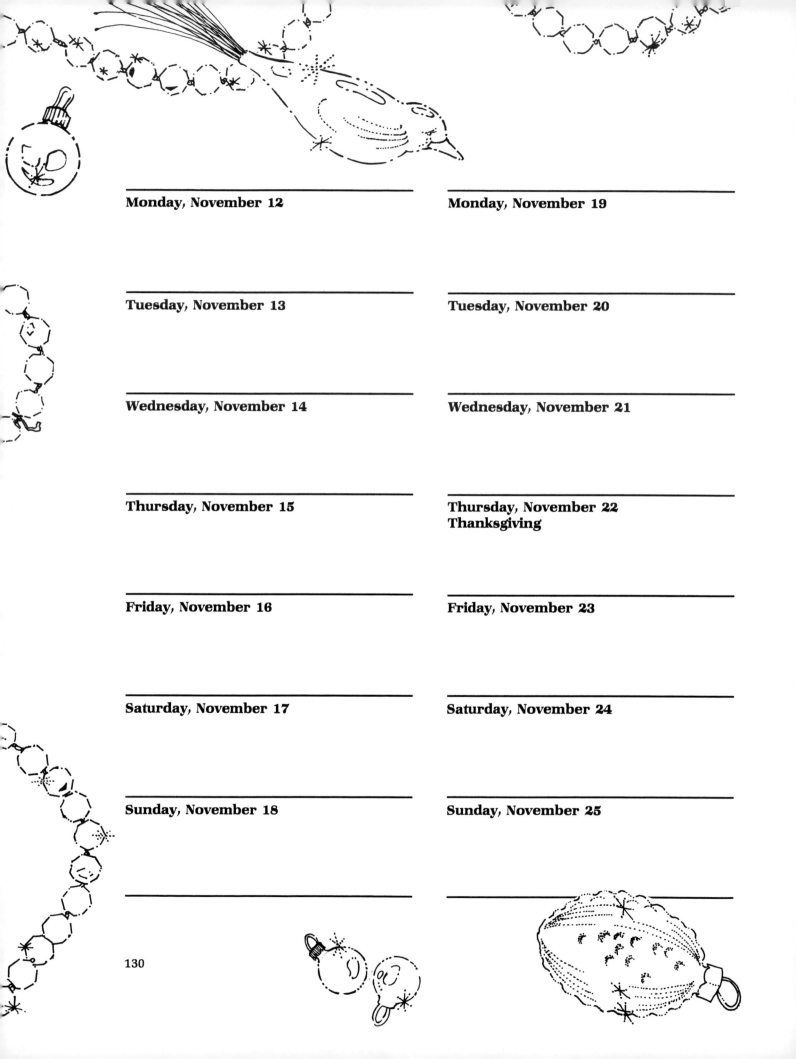

Monday, November 12

Monday, November 19

Tuesday, November 13

Tuesday, November 20

Wednesday, November 14

Wednesday, November 21

Thursday, November 15

Thursday, November 22
Thanksgiving

Friday, November 16

Friday, November 23

Saturday, November 17

Saturday, November 24

Sunday, November 18

Sunday, November 25

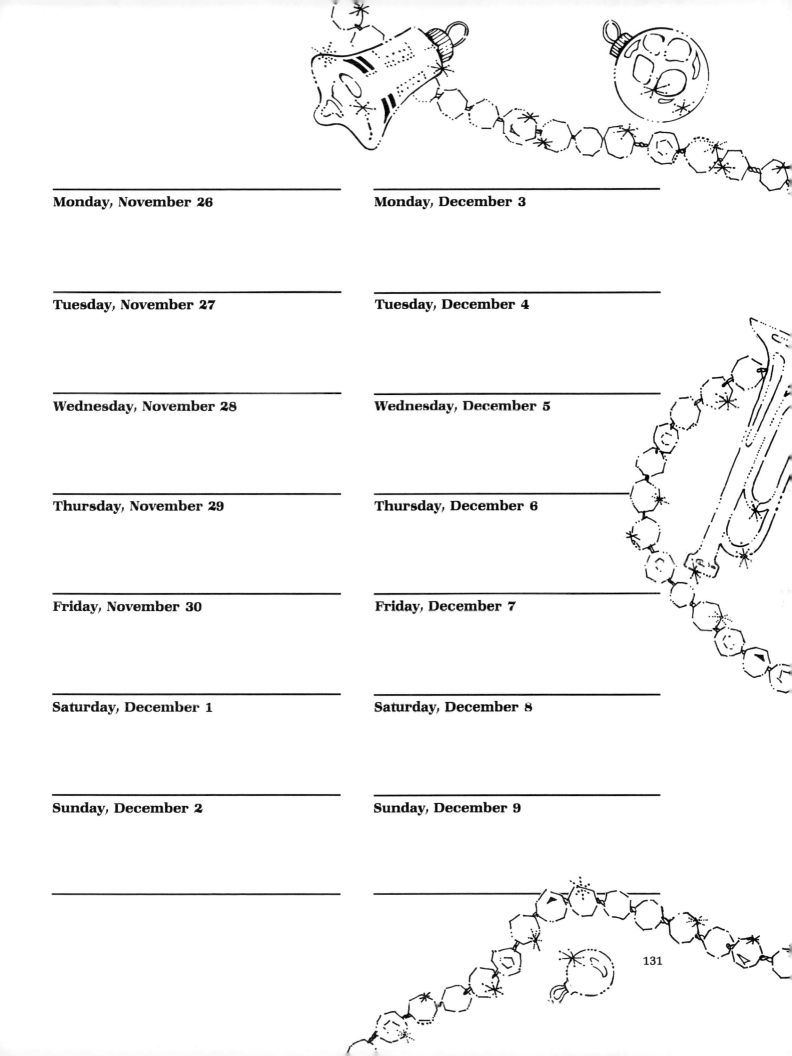

Monday, November 26

Tuesday, November 27

Wednesday, November 28

Thursday, November 29

Friday, November 30

Saturday, December 1

Sunday, December 2

Monday, December 3

Tuesday, December 4

Wednesday, December 5

Thursday, December 6

Friday, December 7

Saturday, December 8

Sunday, December 9

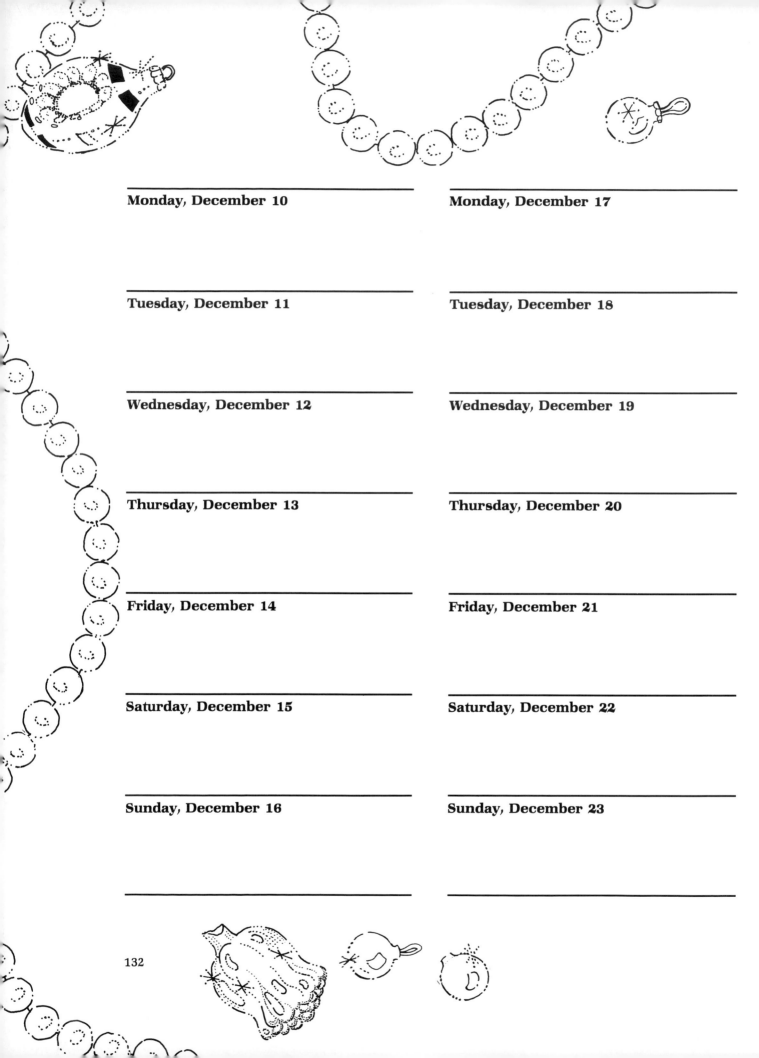

Monday, December 10

Tuesday, December 11

Wednesday, December 12

Thursday, December 13

Friday, December 14

Saturday, December 15

Sunday, December 16

Monday, December 17

Tuesday, December 18

Wednesday, December 19

Thursday, December 20

Friday, December 21

Saturday, December 22

Sunday, December 23

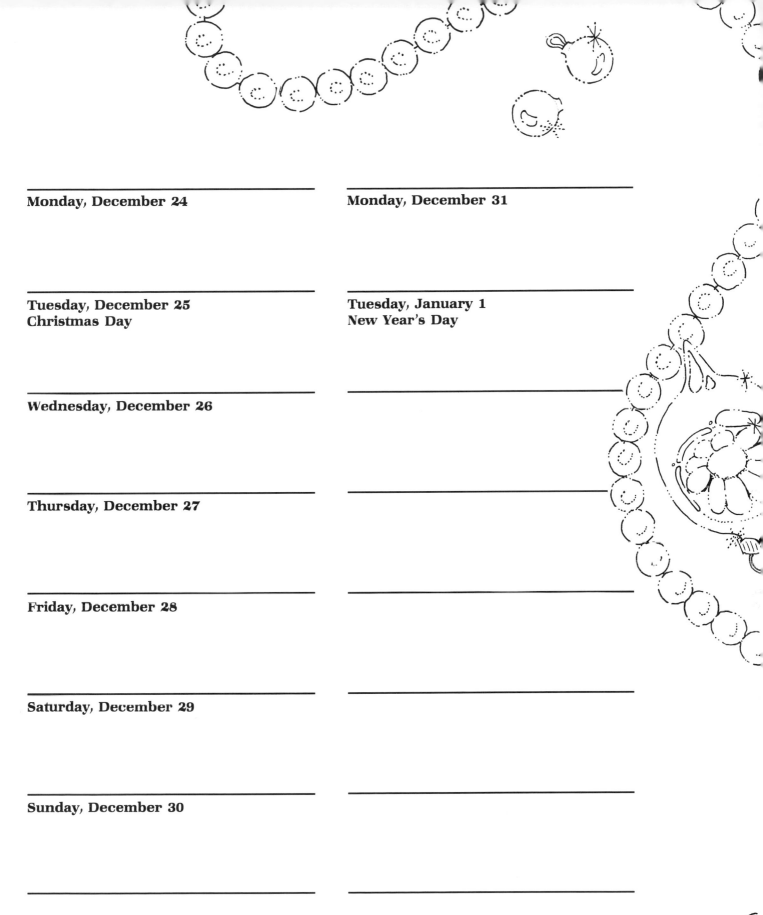

Monday, December 24

Tuesday, December 25
Christmas Day

Wednesday, December 26

Thursday, December 27

Friday, December 28

Saturday, December 29

Sunday, December 30

Monday, December 31

Tuesday, January 1
New Year's Day

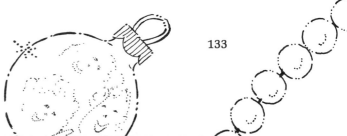

Party Planning

The best-planned parties are the best parties. The traditions of Christmas and of Southern hospitality blend naturally into special entertaining during the holidays. Use the planner given here as a practical approach to a joyous holiday event.

SCHEDULING THE PARTY

Begin by listing parties you will give during the holidays. Plan the time for each party, checking schedules with family members. When will your holiday decorations go up? How long will they last? How can you take advantage of their freshness? Will you have house guests during the holidays? Would it be easier to entertain a large group before the house guests arrive? Describe the size and the type of party (buffet, dinner, brunch) and the degree of formality.

MAKING THE GUEST LIST

Who will you invite? How many? How will you arrange for the comfort of the guests with seating and moving about? Does one of the guests particularly enjoy a dish you make? Do you know the drink preferences of guests? If you know that a guest is allergic to a food, you will want to avoid that food or quietly offer a choice.

SELECTING THE MENU

List the foods you would like to consider, along with cookbooks and page numbers for the recipes. Imagine the food on the plate. Are the dishes attractive together? Consider the cooking time. Do two dishes require the use of the oven at the same time but at different temperatures? Are there two sauces that require constant stirring minutes before serving? What can you prepare ahead? Consider the budget; if necessary, switch to a more moderately priced food and serve plenty of it.

PLANNING THE TABLESETTING

Will you use one table or more? Where can you set up extra tables? Will you serve from a buffet or at the table? Which china, glassware, and serving dishes will you use? Are the holiday linens packed away? Will they need freshening for the party? Does silver need polishing? What will you use as a centerpiece? Can it be made ahead, or can you assemble the container and other supplies you will need? Just before the guests arrive, take a snapshot of the table setting and of the centerpieces to keep for future planning.

ARRANGING SPECIAL TOUCHES

What can you do to make this party different from other parties? Consider a handmade ornament atop a napkin, a centerpiece that is particularly festive, candles with red bows on the candleholders. If gifts will be exchanged, plan a time for this. Select the albums for the stereo. Do not forget fresh towels for the bathroom that guests will use.

READY, SET, GO

Remember that food and decorations are only a part of the party; friendliness and a relaxed attitude are essential to hospitality. Plan as far ahead as possible. Purchase everything—from candles to whipped cream—in advance. The party is sure to be a success, because you have thought it through beforehand and you are prepared.

EVALUATING THE PARTY

After the party, always evaluate it as a whole, and then examine the various parts of the party. Was one dish more trouble than it was worth? Was one dish spectacular? Did a guest mention a particular food? Were there any scheduling problems? What would you repeat for another party? What would you change? Record what you wore as a reference for the next party you will plan for the holidays and for entertaining this group.

Party Planner

Occasion: _____   Number of people: _____

Description: _____   Date/Time: _____

Guest List:

_____   _____

_____   _____

_____   _____

_____   _____

_____   _____

_____   _____

_____   _____

_____   _____

Table Service: Where will you serve? _____

Tables		Chairs	
Tablecloth		Napkins	
Buffet Runner		Napkin Rings	
Centerpiece		Candles	
China		Silver	
Glassware		Favors	

Menu: Dish   Cookbook   Page Number

_____

_____

_____

_____

_____

_____

_____

_____

Remarks:

Party Planner

Occasion: _____   Number of people: _____

Description: _____   Date/Time: _____

Guest List: _____   _____

_____   _____

_____   _____

_____   _____

_____   _____

_____   _____

_____   _____

_____   _____

_____   _____

Table Service: Where will you serve? _____

Tables _____   Chairs _____

Tablecloth _____   Napkins _____

Buffet Runner _____   Napkin Rings _____

Centerpiece _____   Candles _____

China _____   Silver _____

Glassware _____   Favors _____

Menu: Dish   Cookbook   Page Number

_____

_____

_____

_____

_____

_____

_____

_____

Remarks:

Patterns

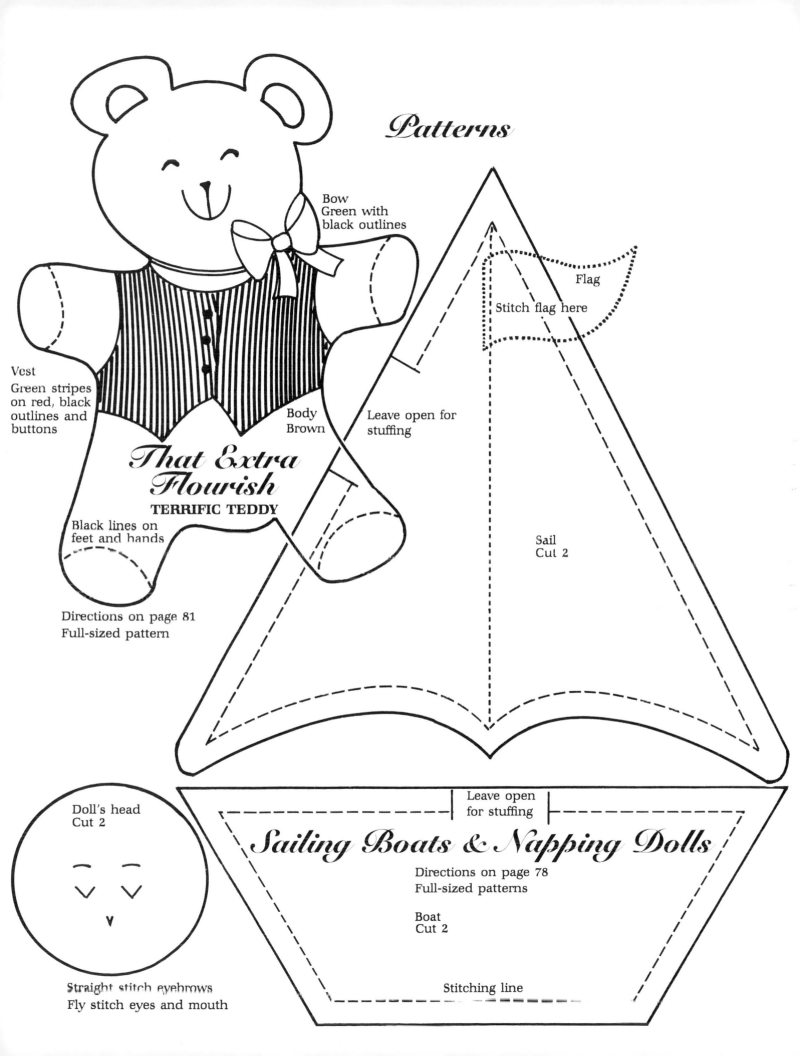

Bow
Green with
black outlines

Vest
Green stripes
on red, black
outlines and
buttons

Body
Brown

Leave open for
stuffing

Flag

Stitch flag here

That Extra Flourish
TERRIFIC TEDDY

Black lines on
feet and hands

Directions on page 81
Full-sized pattern

Sail
Cut 2

Leave open
for stuffing

Doll's head
Cut 2

Sailing Boats & Napping Dolls

Directions on page 78
Full-sized patterns

Boat
Cut 2

Straight stitch eyebrows
Fly stitch eyes and mouth

Stitching line

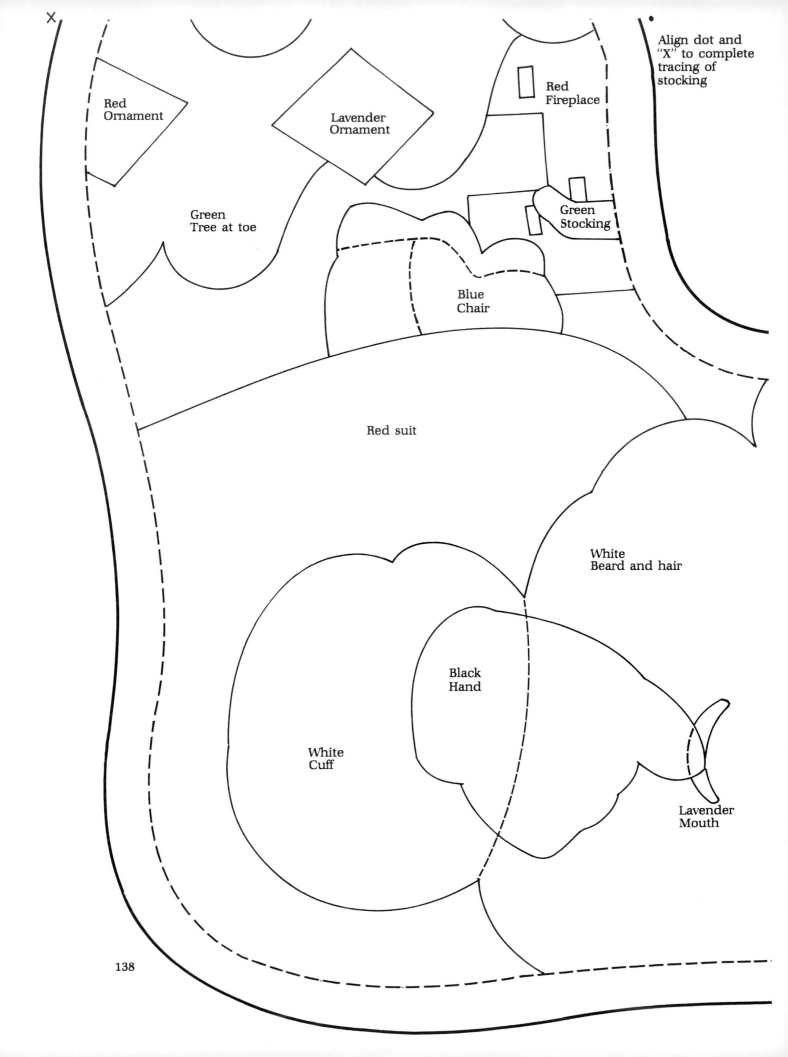

X

Align dot and "X" to complete tracing of stocking

Red Ornament

Lavender Ornament

Red Fireplace

Green Tree at toe

Green Stocking

Blue Chair

Red suit

White Beard and hair

Black Hand

White Cuff

Lavender Mouth

138

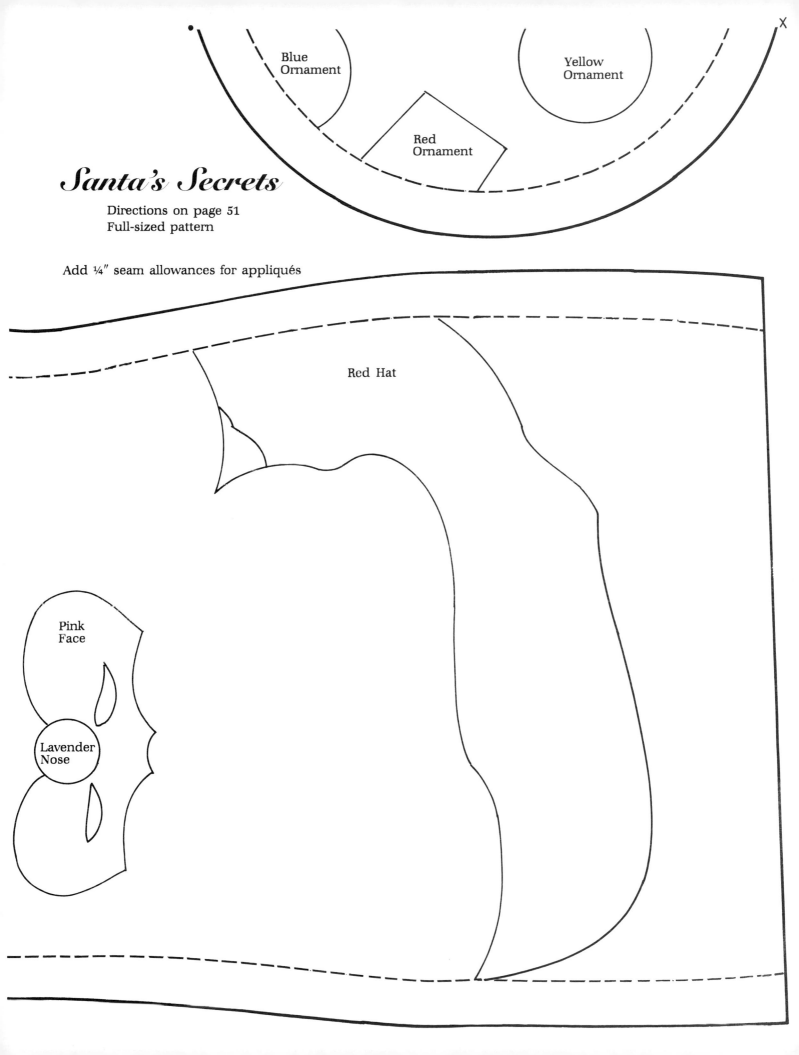

X

Blue
Ornament

Yellow
Ornament

Red
Ornament

Santa's Secrets

Directions on page 51
Full-sized pattern

Add ¼″ seam allowances for appliqués

Red Hat

Pink
Face

Lavender
Nose

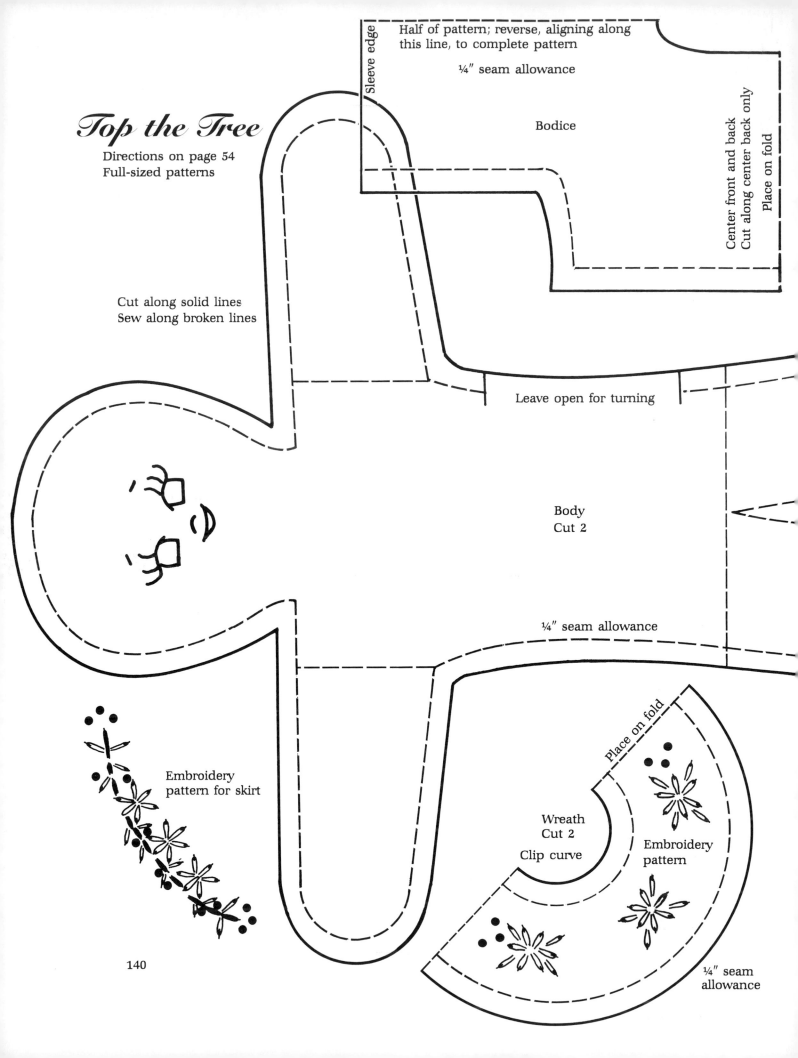

Top the Tree

Directions on page 54
Full-sized patterns

Cut along solid lines
Sew along broken lines

Sleeve edge

Half of pattern; reverse, aligning along
this line, to complete pattern

¼″ seam allowance

Bodice

Center front and back
Cut along center back only
Place on fold

Leave open for turning

Body
Cut 2

¼″ seam allowance

Embroidery
pattern for skirt

Place on fold

Wreath
Cut 2

Clip curve

Embroidery
pattern

¼″ seam
allowance

140

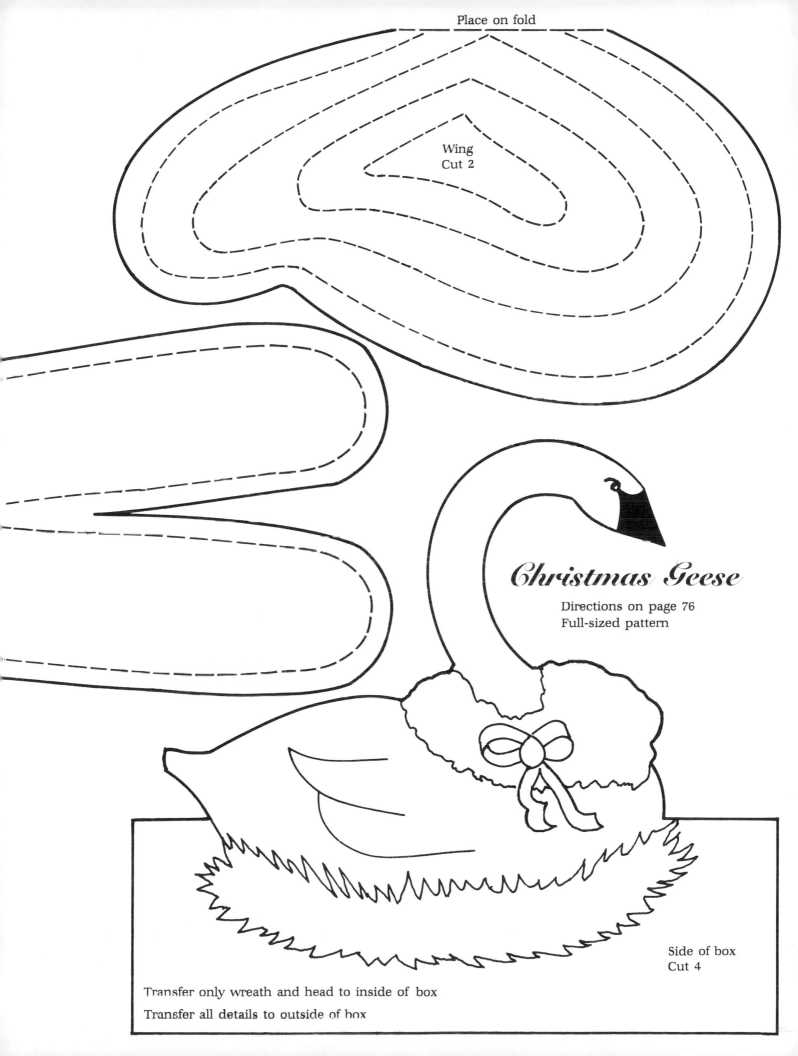

Place on fold

Wing
Cut 2

Christmas Geese

Directions on page 76
Full-sized pattern

Side of box
Cut 4

Transfer only wreath and head to inside of box

Transfer all details to outside of box

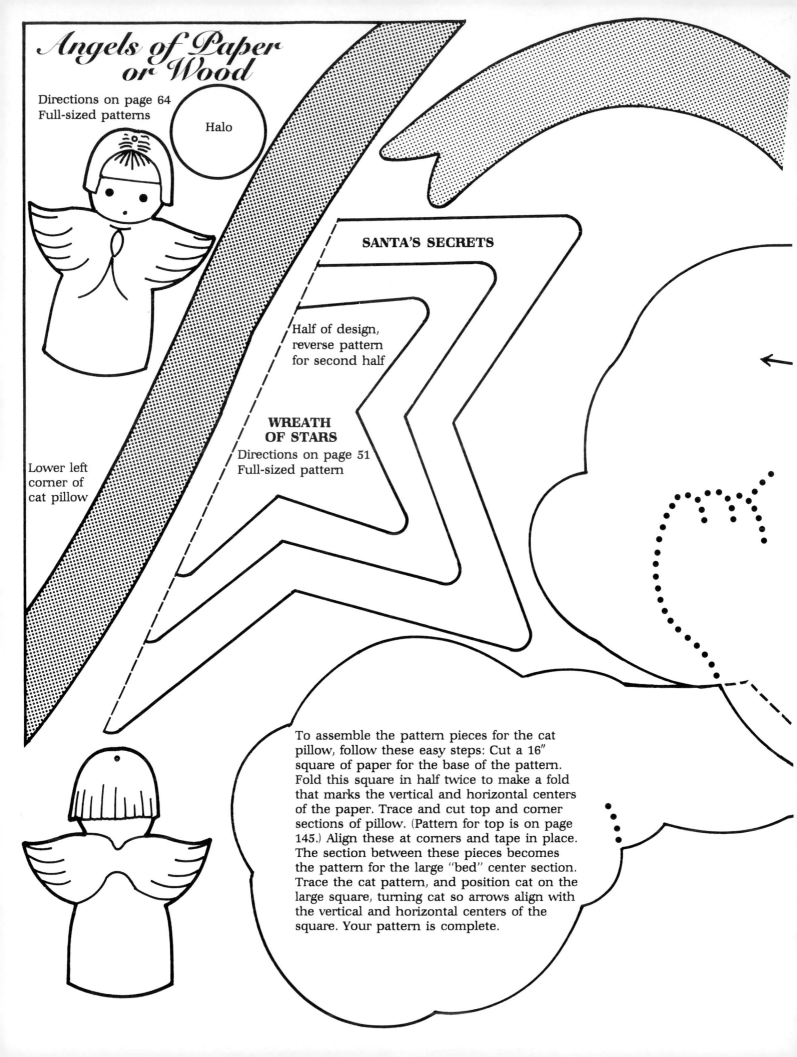

Angels of Paper or Wood

Directions on page 64
Full-sized patterns

Halo

Lower left
corner of
cat pillow

SANTA'S SECRETS

Half of design,
reverse pattern
for second half

**WREATH
OF STARS**

Directions on page 51
Full-sized pattern

To assemble the pattern pieces for the cat
pillow, follow these easy steps: Cut a 16"
square of paper for the base of the pattern.
Fold this square in half twice to make a fold
that marks the vertical and horizontal centers
of the paper. Trace and cut top and corner
sections of pillow. (Pattern for top is on page
145.) Align these at corners and tape in place.
The section between these pieces becomes
the pattern for the large "bed" center section.
Trace the cat pattern, and position cat on the
large square, turning cat so arrows align with
the vertical and horizontal centers of the
square. Your pattern is complete.

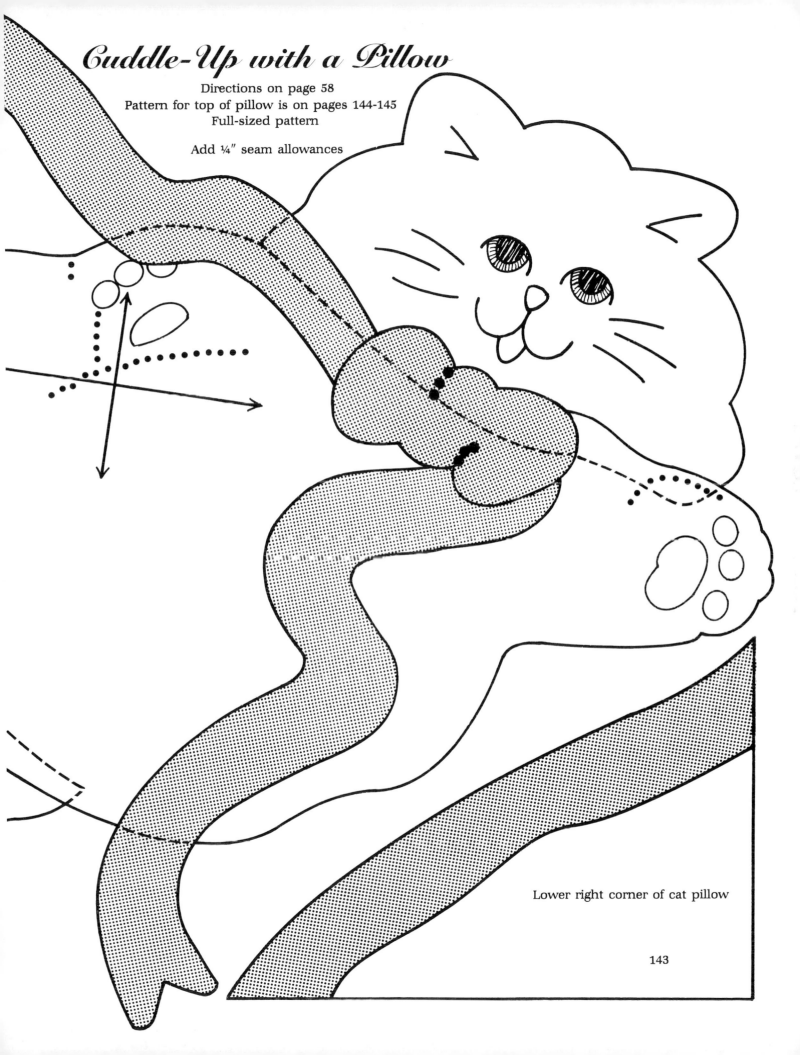

Cuddle-Up with a Pillow

Directions on page 58
Pattern for top of pillow is on pages 144-145
Full-sized pattern

Add ¼" seam allowances

Lower right corner of cat pillow

143

CUDDLE-UP WITH A PILLOW

Remaining pattern pieces on pages 142-143

Top of pillow

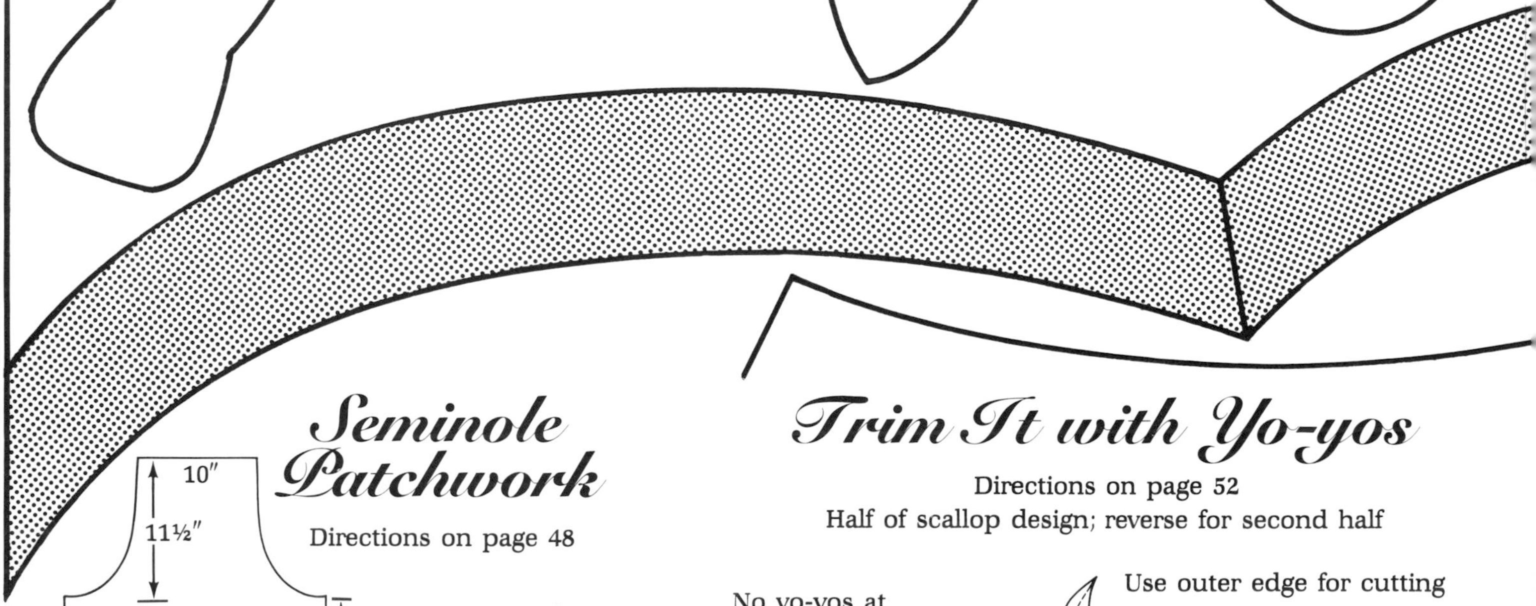

Holiday Carousel

Directions on page 44
Full-sized patterns

Add ¼″ seam allowances

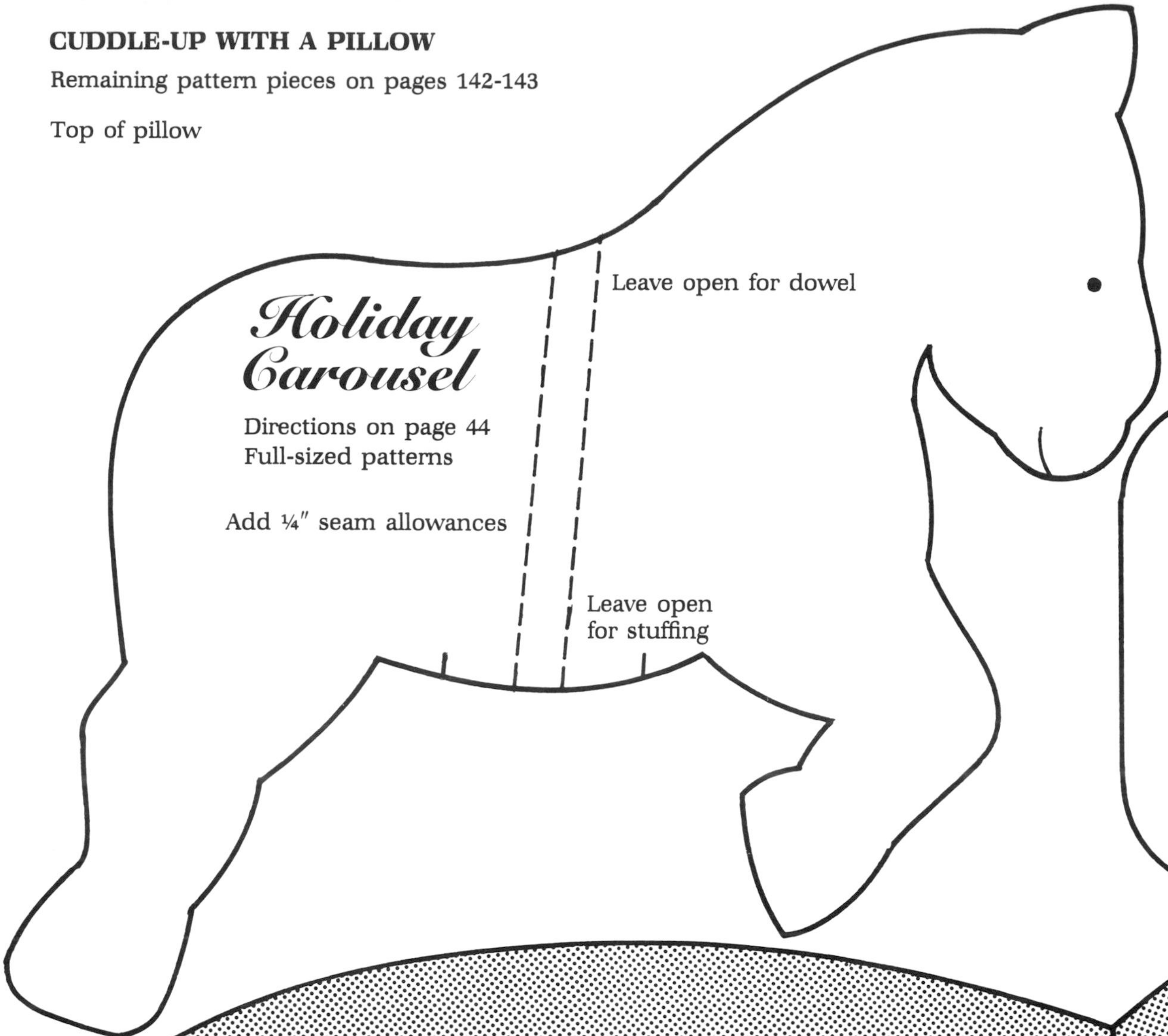

Leave open for dowel

Leave open
for stuffing

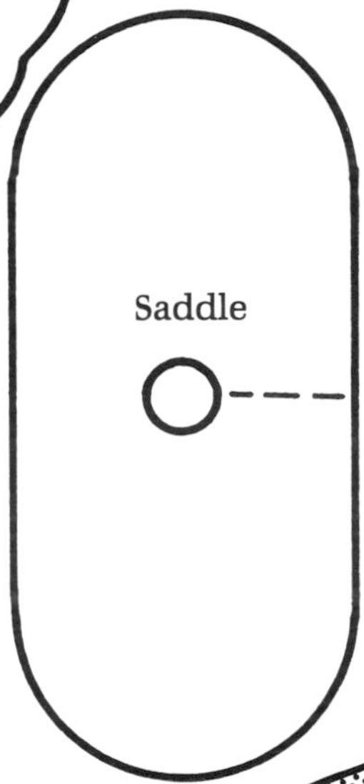

Saddle

Seminole Patchwork

Directions on page 48

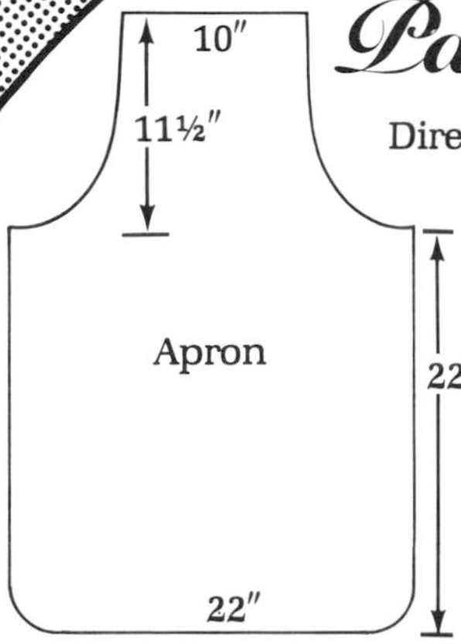

10″

11½″

Apron

22″

22″

22″

Trim It with Yo-yos

Directions on page 52
Half of scallop design; reverse for second half

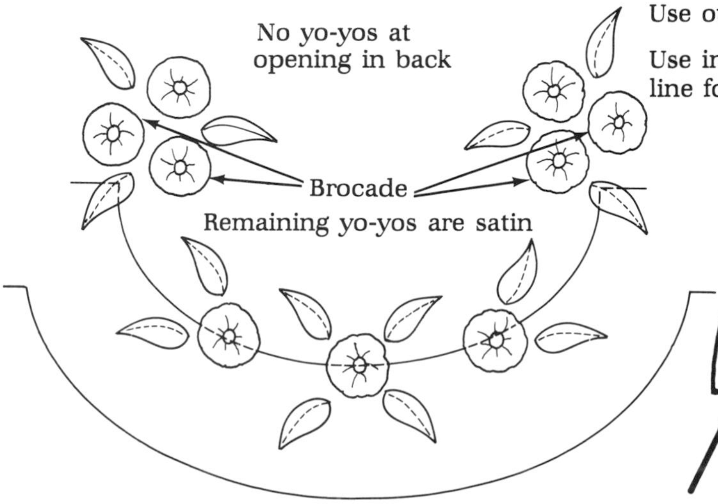

No yo-yos at
opening in back

Use outer edge for cutting

Use inner edge to mark
line for trim

Brocade

Remaining yo-yos are satin

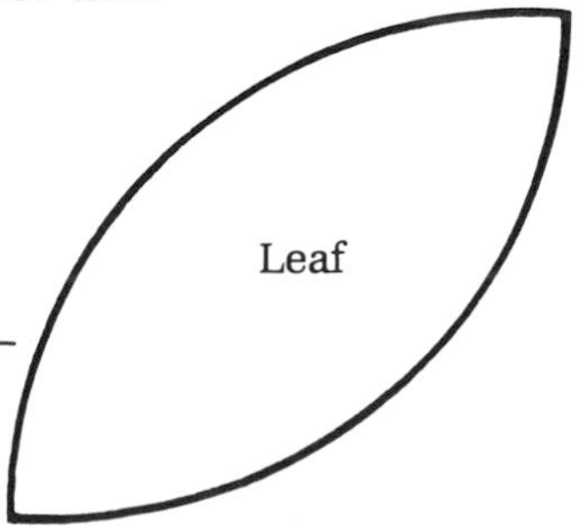

Leaf

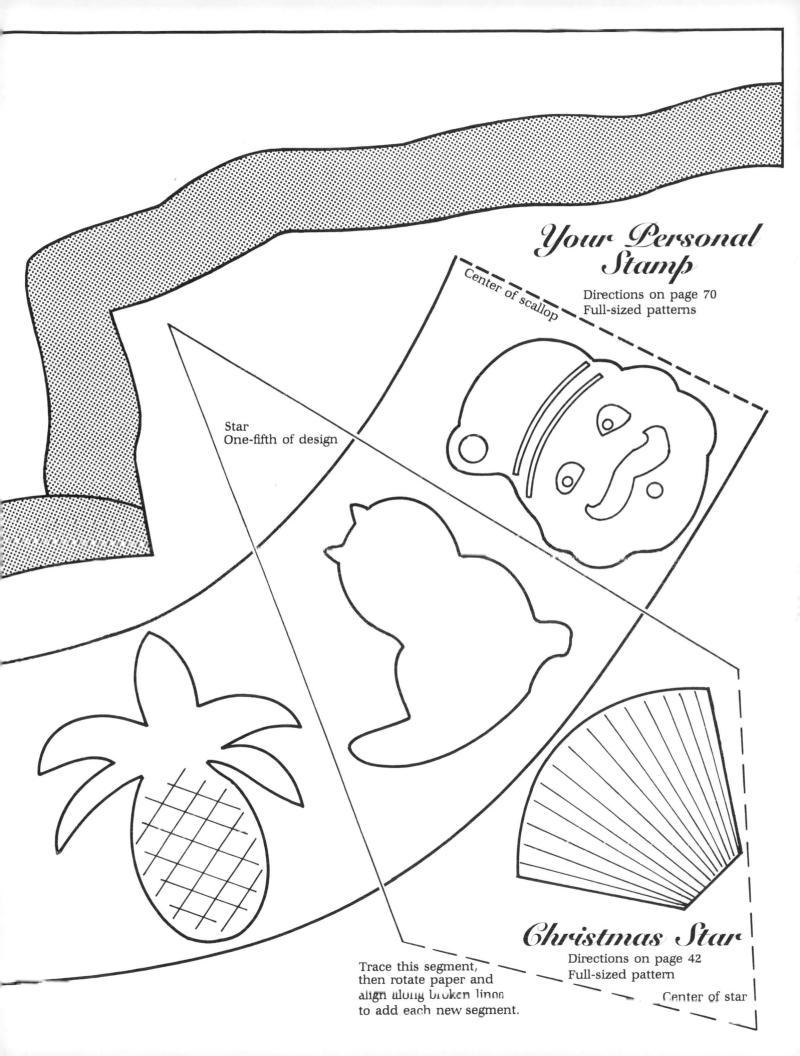

Your Personal Stamp

Center of scallop

Directions on page 70
Full-sized patterns

Star
One-fifth of design

Christmas Star

Directions on page 42
Full-sized pattern

Center of star

Trace this segment,
then rotate paper and
align along broken lines
to add each new segment.

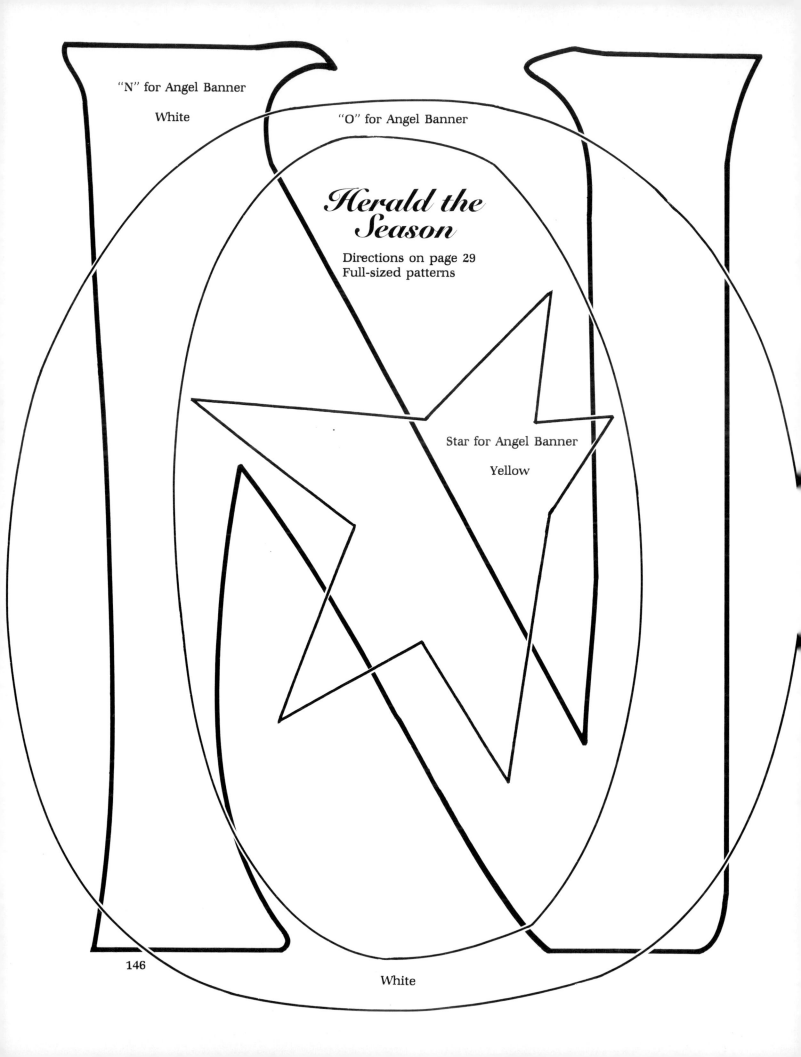

"N" for Angel Banner

White

"O" for Angel Banner

Herald the Season

Directions on page 29
Full-sized patterns

Star for Angel Banner

Yellow

146

White

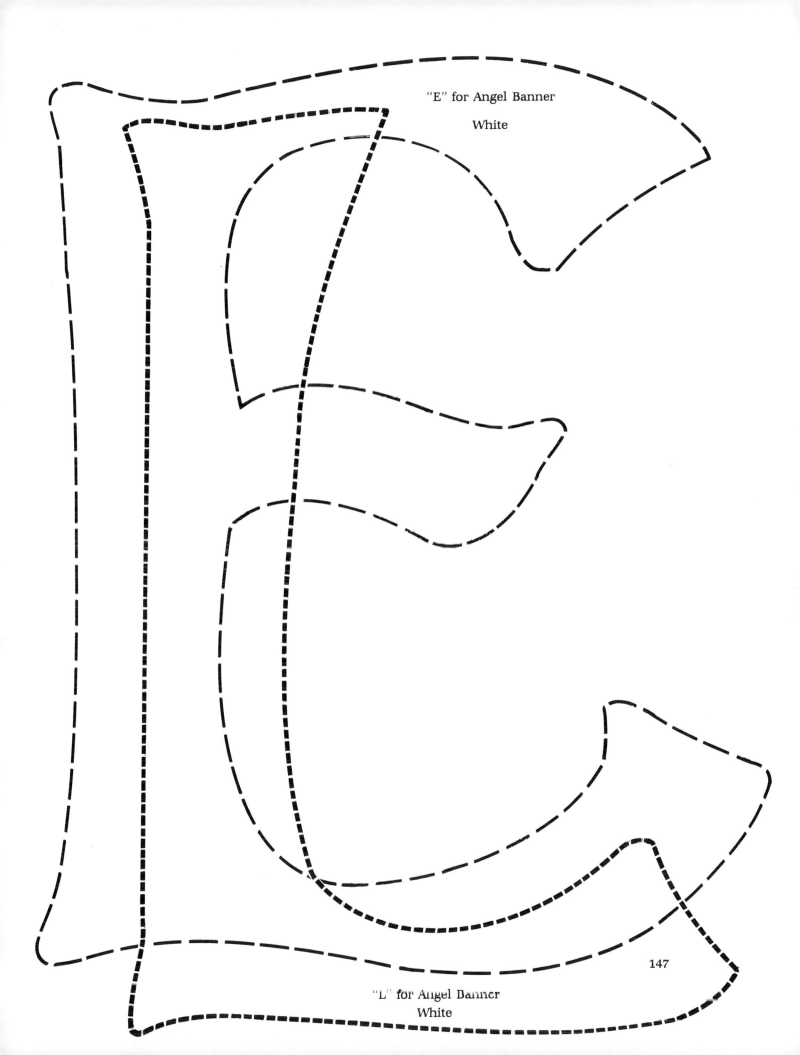

"E" for Angel Banner

White

"L" for Angel Banner

White

147

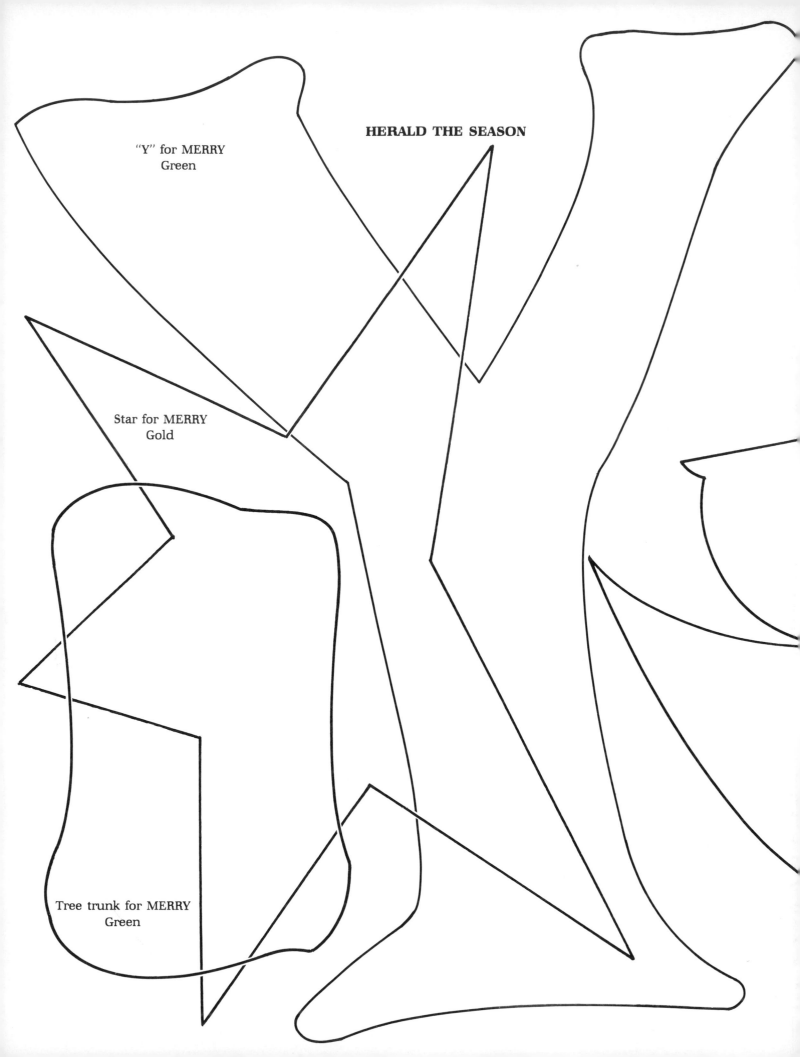

HERALD THE SEASON

"Y" for MERRY
Green

Star for MERRY
Gold

Tree trunk for MERRY
Green

Halo
White

Cut hair, face, and
neck in one piece

Hair and facial features
are painted

Head
Flesh-colored
fabric

Wing
Yellow

Collar
White

Hands
Flesh

Bodice
Red

Cut bodice and sleeves in one piece

Crescent
White

Skirt and feet
Yellow

Cut skirt and feet in one piece

149

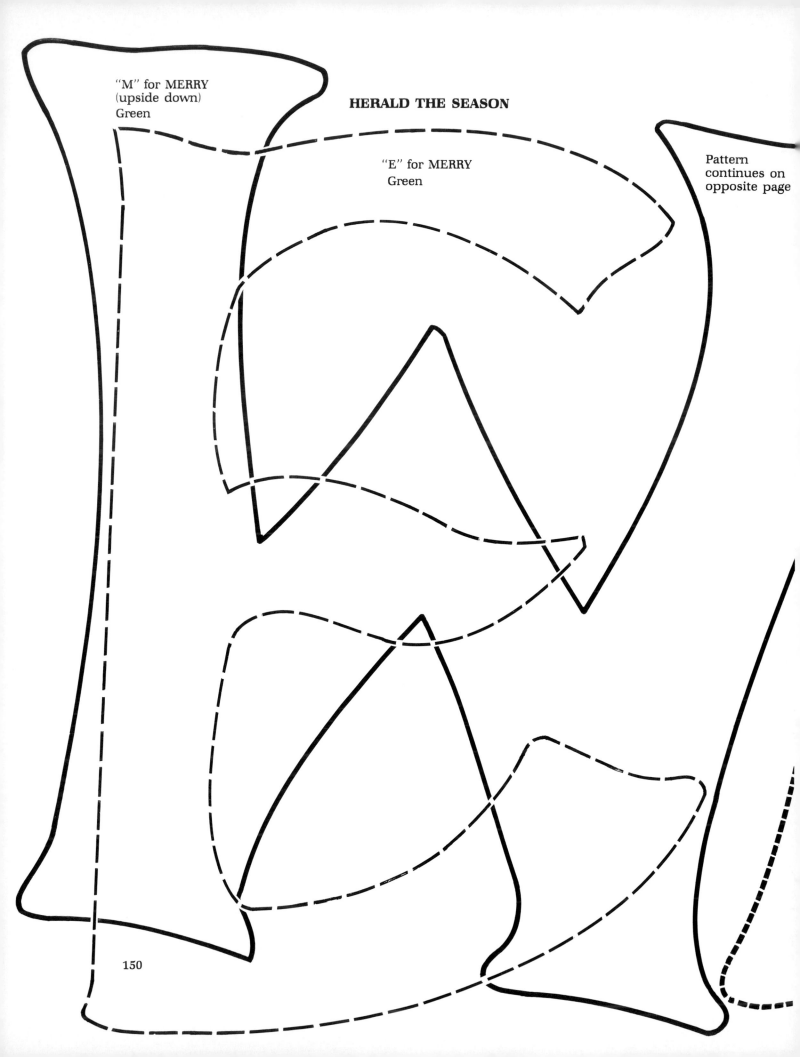

"M" for MERRY
(upside down)
Green

HERALD THE SEASON

"E" for MERRY
Green

Pattern
continues on
opposite page

150

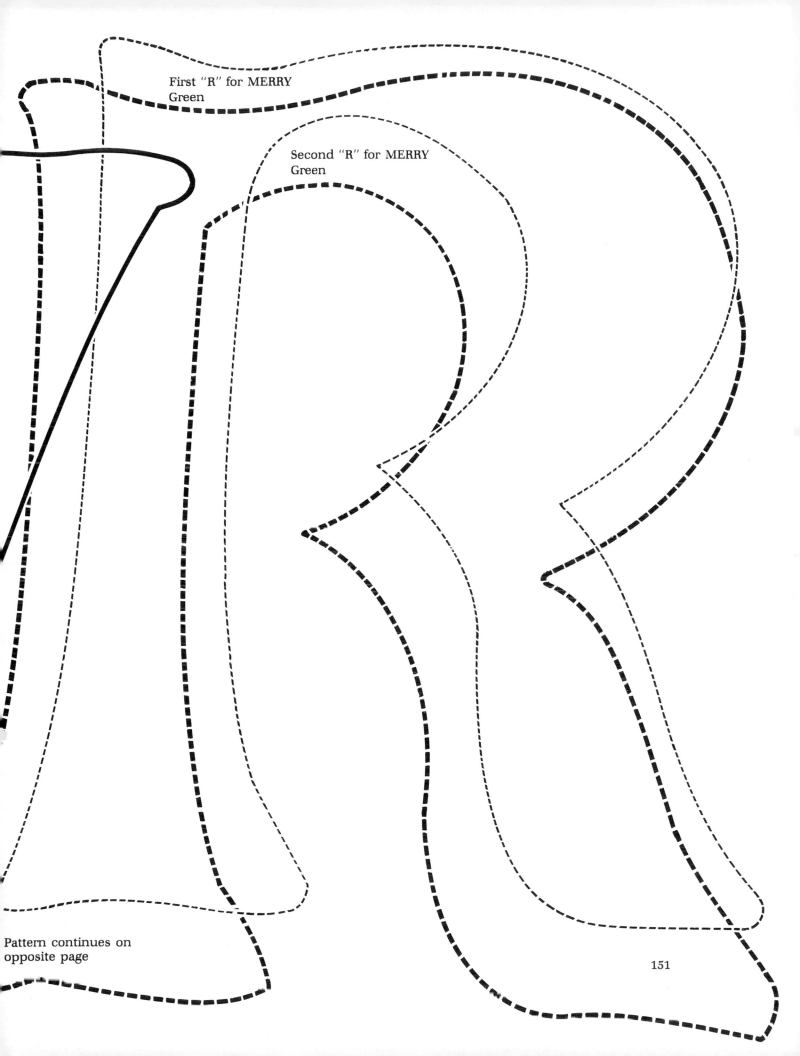

First "R" for MERRY
Green

Second "R" for MERRY
Green

Pattern continues on
opposite page

151

Cross-Stitch on Stockings

Directions on page 70
Full-sized patterns

Alphabet
for stocking

Color Key:
☒ red
◉ dark green
⊘ light green

Backstitch
around
berries and
bow with dark
green

Wreath for stocking

How Many Days?

Directions on page 77

Color Key: DMC Numbers

◼ 3371 black
☐ 712 white
◪ 961 dark pink
◪ 963 pink
· 435 light brown
◉ 433 medium brown
● 666 red
◣ 699 green
◹ 725 golden yellow

½″ seam allowance

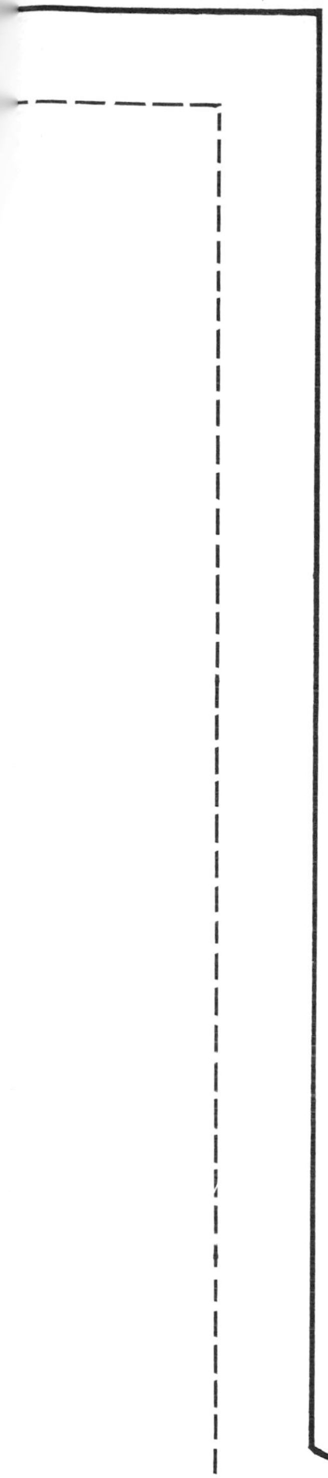

Frame Your Favorites

Directions on page 69

Color Key:
⊠ red
⊡ green

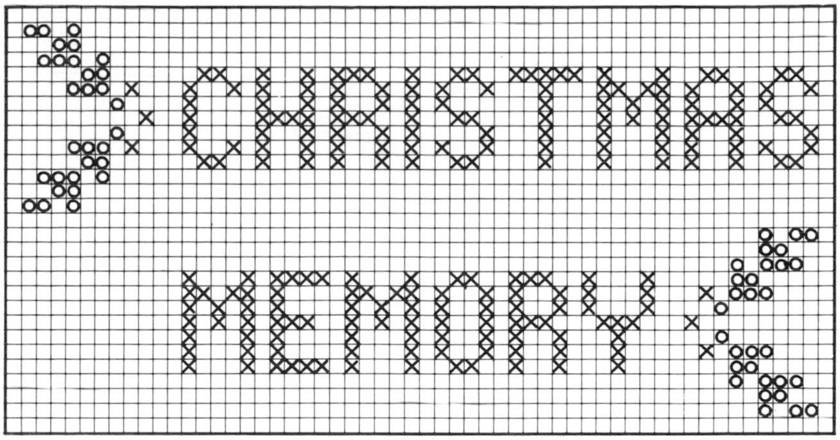

CHRISTMAS MEMORY

To complete stocking pattern, trace from top of stocking to bottom of page; then add heel at bottom of tracing. Toe is cut separately from Aida.

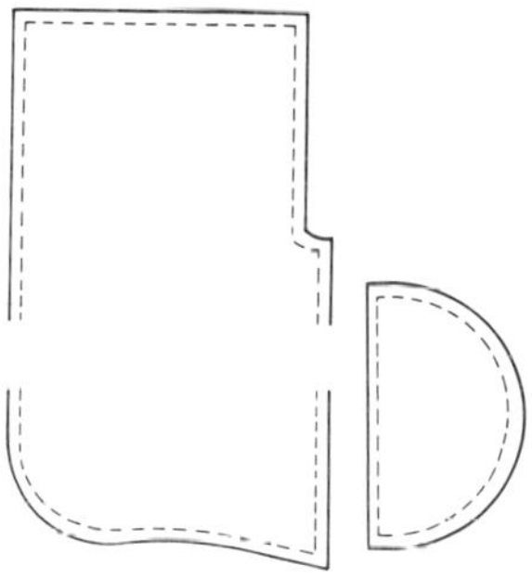

Heel of stocking

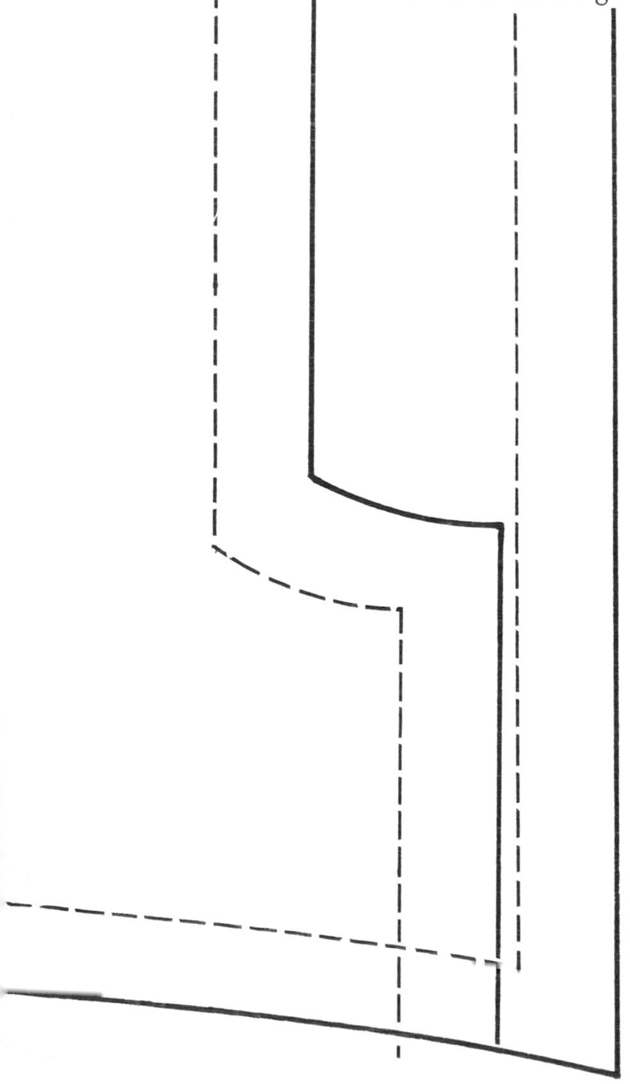

Toe of stocking

THAT EXTRA FLOURISH

SANTA BAGS
Directions on page 81
Full-sized pattern

Cut red hat, white head, pink face, bright pink nose and mouth, black glove

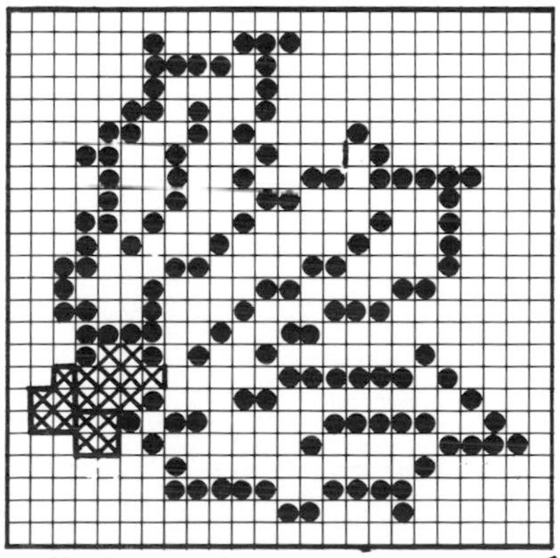

Color key on opposite page

fill in with light green

Holly leaves for stocking

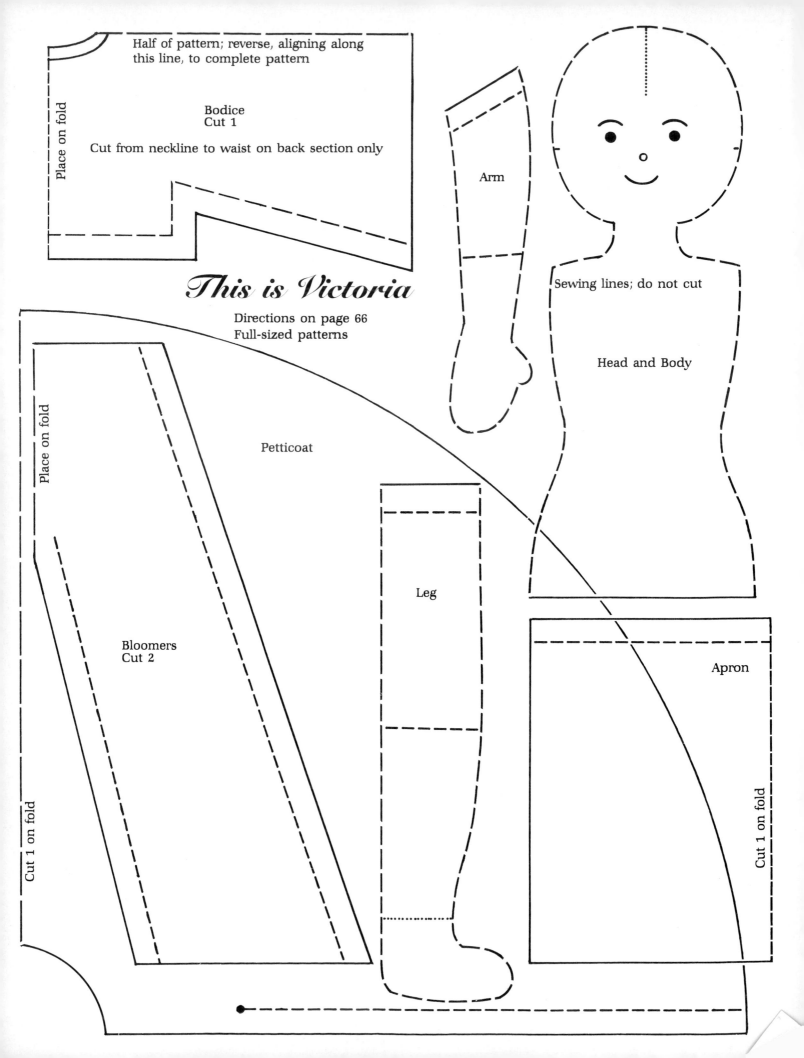

Half of pattern; reverse, aligning along this line, to complete pattern

Place on fold

Bodice
Cut 1

Cut from neckline to waist on back section only

Arm

Sewing lines; do not cut

Head and Body

This is Victoria

Directions on page 66
Full-sized patterns

Place on fold

Petticoat

Leg

Bloomers
Cut 2

Apron

Cut 1 on fold

Cut 1 on fold

Contributors

Design: Carol Middleton
Editorial Assistant: Lisa Gant
Assistance, proofing: Becky Brennan
Production: Jerry Higdon, Jane Bonds,
 Jim Thomas
Art: Carol Middleton, David Morrison,
 Don Smith
Art Director: Bob Nance

Special thanks to the following people from
Southern Living: Jean Wickstrom Liles,
Foods Editor; Lynn Lloyd, Former Test
Kitchens Director; Diane Hogan, Test Kitchens Home Economist; Beverly Morrow,
Foods Photo Stylist; and Vann Cleveland,
Director of Photography.

DESIGNERS

Jeffrey K. Adkisson, lights in ivy 15.
Edward Armstrong, wreath on lighthouse 19.
Viola Andrycich, tree ornament 75.
Dorinda Beaumont, tree skirt and yo-yo ornaments 52-53.
Rita Martinez de Blake, strawberry 60-61.
Jeannine Burge, mailbox 34.
Candace N. Conard and Lindsay Franklin, collectors tree 24-25.
Frances B. Cook, bread dough scenes 62.
Donna C. Cooley, stockings 70.
Anna Mary Duckworth, goose box 76.
Lisa Gant, wreath of moneyplant 36, stamps 70.
Martha Haarbauer, mantel 26-27, flower arrangement in candleholder 40.
Beth Hamilton, walnut ornaments 82.
Brenda Blevins Hammond, tree topper 54.
Ann A. Harrison, banners 28-30
Gerry Hedberg, angels 64.
Dora Hooks, winter magnolias 38, base for greenery 40-41, star 42, pineapple of yucca 43.
Patricia J. Horton, frame 69, How Many Days 77, casserole cover 80.
Linda Johnson and Martha Walthall, floorcloth 30.
Helen H. Kittinger, bird feeder 73.
Priscilla A. Lange, pinecone ornament 60-61.

Deborah Carter Leland, carousel horses 44-45.
Posy Baker Lough, bell ornament 60-61.
Susan Hoyt McCay, boat and doll 78.
Candy McMillan, kitchen with bows 24.
Carol Middleton, Santa stocking 50, cat pillows 58, felt Santas 81. Drawings of Lazy Kitty© Carol Middleton.
Mary Catharine Nicol, gingerbread boy 72.
Sunny O'Neil, Victorian leaf wreath 37.
Cathy Page Pentz, small wreaths 64.
Teri Phillips, wreath in cottage 18, mantel decoration 20, tree and garland 21.
Judy R. Sims, Victorian doll 66.
J. Michael Smith, floral arrangement 14.
Shelley Stewart, garland of pine 33, foliage cluster beneath light 40, cookie jar lid 81.
Heather Ticheli, napkin ring 74.
Carol M. Tipton, Seminole patchwork runner, apron, hotpads 46-48.
Jo Voce, card table cover and bows 35, Curly-Q wreath 48, wreath of stars 51, bows and tassels 53, ribbon and lace ornaments 53 and 56.
Michael Walls, tree with poinsettias 32, garland of magnolias 33, arrangements in moose and hen containers 34.

PHOTOGRAPHERS

Katherine Adams, 14, top left 15, bottom 15, 18, 19, 20, 21, 22, 64.
Jim Bathie, bottom 24, 37, left 40, right 63, 76, 82.
Mike Clemmer, top and center 24, 25.
Frederica Georgia, 10, 11, 12, 13.
Jim Hagans, top right 15.
Mary-Gray Hunter, 16, 17, 36, 41, 51, bottom 55, 59, 66, 70, 71, 72, left 73, bottom 75, 79, 80.
Helen H. Kittinger, right 73.
Bob Lancaster, 38, 39, bottom 42, 77.
Beth Maynor, 31, 32, right 33, top left and right 34, bottom right 40, top 42, 44, 45, 48, 49, 52, 53, 56, 58, 60, 61, left 63, 65, 67, 78.
John O'Hagan, 4, 5, 6, 7, 8, 9, 26-27, 28, 30, left 33, bottom 34, 35, top right 40, 43, 46, 50, top 55, 69, top 75.
Charles E. Walton, cover, title page, contents, 1, 2-3, 23, 57, 83, 84, 85, 86, 88, 91, 94, 97, 100, 103, 104, 106, 110, 111, 115, 118, 121, 122, 123.